# THE COMPLETE AIR FRYER COOKBOOK

# THE COMPLETE AIR FRYER

140 super-easy,
everyday recipes
and techniques

**Sam & Dom Milner**
of RecipeThis

COOKBOOK

WHITE LION PUBLISHING

# Quarto

First published in 2023 by White Lion Publishing
an imprint of The Quarto Group.
One Triptych Place,
London,
SE1 9SH
United Kingdom
T (0)20 7700 6700
www.Quarto.com

A catalogue record for this book is available from the
British Library.

HB ISBN 978 0 7112 8759 4
PB ISBN 978 0 7112 8760 0
Ebook ISBN 978 0 7112 8761 7

10 9 8 7 6 5 4 3 2 1

**Designer:** Georgie Hewitt
**Project Editor:** Rebecca Woods
**Food and Prop Stylist:** Rebecca Woods

Printed in China

## Notes

- All calorie counts are per serving where a recipe states "Serves" or per item when a recipe states "Makes"
- All milk should be whole/full-fat unless otherwise stated
- All eggs should be UK large eggs or US XL eggs, unless otherwise stated
- When baking sweet treats, we recommend unsalted butter, and in savoury cooking salted butter. Unless otherwise stated, bring the butter to room temperature before using.
- Do refer to your air fryer manual as they often operate differently and follow the manufacturer's safety guidelines.
- Metric and imperial measurements are given for all recipes, use one set only and not a mixture of both
- All tablespoons and teaspoons are level

# Contents

# WELCOME

I remember it as if it were was yesterday. It was late 2012 and we had come back from a five-week summer holiday in the USA. We had eaten too many burgers and doughnuts and were on the post-holiday diet.

Just by chance, I saw the Philips air fryer advertised in a diet magazine I was flicking through. I showed it to Dom and he took a bit of convincing that a kitchen gadget could produce perfect crispy chips for the calories of a jacket potato. But I won him over and a week later we were paying for our first air fryer in an electronics store.

We took it home and we went straight online to look for air fryer ideas  – and for how to make these chips a reality. There were just two results, both written in German.

Because we were very early to air frying, we realised that we were on our own and that we were going to be the guinea pigs. We made mistakes, we had amazing breakthroughs, and over time we created a catalogue of our favourite air fryer recipes. Three years on, we created RecipeThis and shared our love for the air fryer with amazing people from around the globe and from all walks of life.

*The Complete Air Fryer Cookbook* is for all our readers who were like us back then: who want a simple solution for their new air fryer but might not know where to start. It is a catalogue of go-to air fryer recipes for every meal – from special occasions such as Christmas, Easter or Thanksgiving, or just for those super-busy weeknights, you're sure to find favourite recipes you can cook time and time again. Plus, we have provided many recipe variations, cooking time lists and step-by-step photos for key recipe techniques to help you master air fryer cooking.

We hope you love the air fryer as much as we do and that it helps to make mealtimes easier for you, the same way it has for us.

**Sam & Dom x**

# everything you need to know

In this chapter we will be running through the basics of getting to know your air fryer, completing the temperature test and air frying for the first time.

# getting to know your air fryer

Just like with any new kitchen gadget you purchase, you first need to get to know your air fryer and understand the bare bones of how it functions. This chapter is all about learning the basics, before diving into our everyday air fryer recipes.

## what is an air fryer?

An air fryer is a hugely popular kitchen gadget that cooks food that would traditionally be fried or oven baked. They are like mini convection ovens, which circulate hot air around the ingredients to really crisp them up. They work at twice the speed of a regular oven because they are smaller and so they warm up much faster. You can forget the long preheat you have to do each time you turn your oven on!

### Who is an air fryer for?

The air fryer was originally for those on a diet, who wanted to eat cheesy chips every day without the deep-fried guilt. Nowadays it feels like the air fryer is for everyone: the widowed pensioner that doesn't like cooking for one and wants an easy solution – or has mobility issues and can't stand for long; the mum that wants quick veggies for dinner and has a million things to do on a busy weeknight; the student going to university for the first time and can't cook; or the family that is worried about the cost of energy bills and knows it's much cheaper to cook with the air fryer.

And for those of you who are using the air fryer for dieting, a healthy lifestyle or to help with high blood pressure or type 2 diabetes, we have included many healthy recipes as well as calorie counts.

### The three main types of air fryer

You will soon discover that there are three different types of air fryers.

There are the models with baskets, which are probably the most common; the oven types, which look like a mini version of a classic oven; and the halogen air fryer, which rotates food in a similar way to a paddle-type air fryer, but is much slower than an air fryer basket. If using a halogen air fryer, when following our recipes please add an extra 30 per cent to the cook time – for example, a 10 minute recipe should take 13 minutes.

Many of our readers follow our air fryer basket recipes with an air fryer oven. Just remember that the top shelf is the hottest (just like an oven) and the rotisserie function is best for roasting meats.

## Which air fryer should you buy?

For best results and ease of use, we recommend that you buy an XL basket-style air fryer with a digital display. Also known as a drawer air fryer, they have enough space to cook a complete meal, or even roast a whole chicken. Because the majority of our air fryer users have a basket type, all the recipes have been written with air fryer baskets in mind.

If you have a dual zone air fryer (with two baskets), you can cook everything in one drawer if it won't be too overcrowded, or simply divide it between both drawers and follow the recipe settings in both zones.

There are also air fryers with functions that we don't find that helpful. Avoid air fryers with an automatic preheat. This means that the air fryer will force you to preheat every time you cook – even if you are simply adding a couple of minutes to the cook time.

We find air fryers that don't have a digital time and temperature setting are not as reliable. These manual air fryers have a dial rather than a digital display and it's not as accurate when setting the cook time.

Also avoid air fryers that have just a tray or drawer and no detachable basket. This makes it harder to clean, and also makes it easy to accidentally burn yourself or tip the oil from the bottom of the air fryer onto your plate.

## The biggest buying mistake

When you're choosing your air fryer, it's logical to assume that an appliance advertised for one to two people will suit a small household. When you get it home, however, you check out the recipes and realise that it is way too small.

In fact, an XL-size air fryer is perfect for one to two people. You can cook salmon and asparagus at the same time, or cook a whole chicken; for a one-person household, that chicken will give you leftovers for the next day.

Dom and I have two kids to feed and find ourselves cooking from two XL air fryers. The ideal air fryer size is either XL for one to two people, or a dual drawer air fryer for a larger household.

## What can I air fry?

You're probably wondering what you can air fry. Well, the easiest way to explain it is to say which cooking methods an air fryer can replace. Most things you can cook in a microwave, barbecue, grill/broiler, toaster, toastie machine, frying pan, wok, deep fat fryer or oven can go into the air fryer. For example, instead of stir-frying veggies in a wok, you can air fry them like we do in our veggie stir-fry (page 115) or toast bread in the air fryer basket (see page 36) rather than placing it in the toaster. Although, when replacing the oven, the food – and the bakeware it is in/on – must, of course, fit in the air fryer.

There are of course the odd exceptions; for example, we wouldn't put freshly battered food in the air fryer because the wet batter just sticks to the air fryer basket. Nor would we cook popcorn in there, as the flying kernels run the risk of getting stuck and damaging the air fryer or starting a fire.

## Do you air fry, bake, or grill?

There are many types of air fryers today offering a variety of functions and buttons, which can be confusing.

Many people ask whether they should press "air fry", "bake" or "grill". Well, these buttons are simply pre-sets and we recommend that you press "air fry". Or manually set the time and temperature as we do on our air fryers.

## How do cooking times compare to the oven?

When you first start air frying you will be shocked by how fast it is. For example, a medium whole chicken is cooked in 45 minutes in the air fryer with no preheat (see page 46), yet instructions on the packaging say to oven bake for 1 hour 45 minutes in a preheated oven.

We recommend that when you get started you follow our cook times, and if trying your own recipe that you halve the oven time and check the food is cooked before serving.

## Is the air fryer easy to clean?

Many people complain about cleaning air fryers, but it's not as bad as you might think. It's actually much easier than cleaning your oven or your usual roasting tins.

If you have cooked something greasy, such as pork chops (page 79) or whole chicken (page 46), then both the air fryer basket and drawer will need to be cleaned with hot soapy water. If it's really bad, you can leave it to soak for 20 minutes.

If you just have crumbs from homemade chicken nuggets (page 66) or fish and chips (page 97), you can just tip out the excess crumbs and wipe it clean with a damp cloth.

We also asked air-fryer cleaning expert Sarah how she performs a deep clean. Her advice is to pour 2.5cm/1 inch of water into the air fryer basket with a dash of washing up liquid, then air fry for 10 minutes at 200°C/400°F – this will help break up any hard-to-clean bits. Rinse and wipe clean and your air fryer is as good as new.

If the outside of your air fryer is lacking its shiny appearance, spray it with a basic anti-bacterial kitchen spray and wipe dry. Avoid stronger chemicals, as they can damage the overall appearance of the air fryer over time.

## Should you preheat the air fryer?

Maybe. On page 17, we will be talking about how well your air fryer performs. If you have a slow air fryer, we recommend a preheat to make it's performance equivalent to that of an average air fryer. But if you have an average or high-performing air fryer, it is only necessary to preheat for a handful of recipes, for example the Homemade Yorkshire Puddings (page 173) which need a very hot air fryer to get the rise.

If you preheat a high-performing air fryer, make sure you reduce the cook time by 3 minutes, otherwise that preheat can result in overcooked food.

To preheat the air fryer, simply cook for 3 minutes at the temperature of the recipe, but make sure no baking parchment or air fryer liners are in the air fryer because they will fly about.

## Do you shake or flip your air fryer food?

You will see some extreme air fryer recipes that call for shaking the food every minute or two and this can really put people off getting an air fryer. The reality is that shaking the food is only necessary once or twice in a 20 minute recipe – that's all that's needed to stop it from sticking. Shaking is also only required in a small amount of recipes, for example those with starchy vegetables, such as potatoes, that are likely to stick together.

To shake the food in the air fryer, remove the basket from the unit, grab the handle and shake the basket, just like how you shake chips/fries in a deep fat fryer. Though, of course, the air fryer will not splash you with hot oil.

It's also a good idea (especially when cooking meat) to turn food for an even cook and to stop the food from drying out. Our air fryer whole chicken (page 46) follows this method: we cook it breast side down, and then flip it breast side up for the second half of the cooking time for that perfect moist chicken. You can also do the same with breaded food for an even toasted look.

## Where should you keep the air fryer?

Common sense comes into practice when positioning the air fryer. There have been instances when people have placed air fryers on top of ovens and the air fryer has melted, or beneath kitchen cupboards that have been damaged by the rising hot air from the air fryer.

We recommend that you make sure there is at least 2.5cm/1 inch of space all around the air fryer when in use. If you keep it on a kitchen worktop that might be easily damaged, place a wooden board under it. We also recommend that any cupboard over it doesn't contain food because the extra warmth can spoil the food. The cupboard above our air fryer is where we keep our measuring jugs and a few plastic containers that we use in the air fryer. Its also recommended that you don't leave it plugged in when not in use.

# air fryer tips

Okay, so you have taken the air fryer out of the box and are about to use it; these are a few things to bear in mind.

**It's an average cook time** Just like with ovens, some air fryers cook food faster than others. We have tested the cook times in our recipes on several air fryers and calculated an average for you. For example, most of our air fryers cook soft-boiled eggs in 11 minutes, but our best air fryer does them in 10 minutes, and our slowest does them in 12 minutes. Therefore, we use 11 minutes as the average. Get to know your air fryer (see pages 17–18) and adapt as necessary.

**Overcrowding changes the cook time** We can cook a portion of Brussels sprouts in just under 15 minutes, yet if we have filled the air fryer with a roast including meat, potatoes and sprouts, the cook time will be over 20 minutes as the hot air doesn't circulate as freely.

**The fork test** You will notice us mentioning this a lot throughout the cookbook. A fork test is an easy way to check that food is cooked, especially potatoes. Simply poke a fork into whatever veggie you may be cooking and if the fork goes in easily it is fork tender – and may just need the temperature increasing to make the food crispy.

**Clean regularly** We recommend keeping up with the cleaning of your air fryer. Compared to the oven, air fryers are very easy to clean and we clean ours along with the other washing up. If you leave fat in the air fryer, for example from burgers, the next time you use your air fryer it may produce a lot of smoke.

**Light food takes off** When we first started air frying, we made a mess in the air fryer many times because of this. If you just add a slice of cheese, for example to melt onto a burger, and don't press it down, the circulating air will move it. That's why, in our air fryer courgette pizza slices (page 159), we recommend pushing the grated cheese into cream cheese to stop it flying off. Another solution is using cocktail sticks/toothpicks to hold larger pieces of food in place – for example, pinning a slice of burger cheese to a burger patty to melt it.

**You can add time, but you can't take it away** Air fryers are much faster than ovens and it's very easy to overcook food in the air fryer. When you are getting started with your air fryer, we recommend that you start with less time, check your food, then add extra time if necessary.

**It's a learning curve** We have been air frying for over ten years, yet we still discover new things. Take your time, experiment and don't quit the air fryer if a recipe goes wrong.

**It went wrong** If an air fryer recipe does go wrong, it's most likely because it has cooked at the wrong temperature, or that your air fryer is much slower than ours. That is why the temperature test on page 18 is so important.

**Air-fryer weaning** Like baby weaning, try a new air fryer recipe every three days. It will take the pressure off air frying every meal and you can wean yourself in the direction of a catalogue of air fryer recipes you love.

**Do you have air fryer fear?** We have met many people that have an air fryer still in its box and are worried that they will either not be very good at using it, or they really don't know where to start.

If this is you, we recommend that you begin by reading this chapter and completing the temperature test. Then start with some of the simplest air fryer recipes in this cookbook such as chicken breasts (page 50) or asparagus (page 152).

# ingredients explained

Now let's talk air fryer ingredients. This will give you a better understanding of the ingredients we have used in the recipes and some easy substitutions you can make. You will note that they are all everyday ingredients that most of us will already have in our kitchens.

## Understanding the ingredients

**Eggs** Unless stated otherwise, we recommend using large UK eggs or extra large US ones.

**Onions** You can use white or brown onions in any recipe that calls for onions, unless red is stated.

**Butter** When baking sweet treats, we recommend unsalted butter, and in savoury cooking we use salted butter. Unless otherwise stated, use softened butter for best results.

**Honey** If used in a recipe that has a long cook time, glazes including honey may burn. Instead, add honey close to the end of cook time. In these recipes, we recommend using clear honey. You can also swap honey for maple syrup, if you prefer.

**Mixed herbs** We love mixed herbs. They are convenient and save you buying lots of different herbs. There are other similar options you can use, such as bouquet garni or Italian seasoning. In the UK its more common to use mixed herbs, whilst in the US Italian seasoning is the more popular choice.

**Meat seasoning** In our kitchen we have many different seasoning blends. From poultry seasonings for wings to pork rub for pork chops or steak seasonings. You can use any pork or chicken seasonings in our recipes that call for poultry seasoning.

## Herbs and spices for air-fryer cooking

We recommend that you use dried herbs for air frying. It avoids fresh herb waste and it also sticks to the food you are air frying better. In this cookbook, you will find that 95 per cent of the seasonings are dried.

These are the dried herbs and spices we recommend you stock up on:

- Oregano
- Basil
- Parsley
- Thyme
- Rosemary
- Sweet paprika
- Ground cumin
- Coriander/cilantro leaf
- Salt and black pepper

We also recommend stocking some mixed seasonings, such as mixed herbs, mixed spice (apple spice), pumpkin spice, taco seasoning and poultry seasoning.

You can buy them already mixed or make your own. If you have a favourite mixed seasoning, you can make it in bulk. When we go travelling, we will often reduce the ingredients to take with us and make ourselves a tub of mixed herbs for the journey.

## Metric or imperial?

Because people who use air fryers live around the globe, you will find both metric and imperial measurements on every recipe. For best results, either stick to just metric or just imperial throughout the recipe.

Also note that when a recipe calls for a teaspoon or a tablespoon, it is levelled unless otherwise stated.

# Using fats and oils in the air fryer

Oil is often such a big topic of conversation with new air fryer users; they want to understand what oils to use, how to use them and if they can go oil free. This page is dedicated to everything oil.

## How much oil do you use?

The main question we get asked about cooking in the air fryer, is about how much oil to use. This, of course, depends on the recipe.

A food that you would normally cook in the oven without adding oil – such as chicken nuggets – usually only needs oil if you want a crisp to the food, but you could go oil free if you wanted to.

A food that you would always add fat or oil to when cooking in the oven – such as a whole chicken, which usually requires butter under the skin – will need a bit of oil to air fry, but much less. In the air fryer it will only need about one tablespoon (depending on chicken size) to cook it and crisp it up.

## Can you go oil-free in the air fryer?

A few years back, there was an air fryer trend of cooking chips/fries without oil. We tried it and they were absolutely awful – the worst chips I had ever eaten. The lesson learnt is that air fryers are all about cooking with less oil, not no oil. You can have a portion of chips with less than a teaspoon of olive oil per serving, but you will often still need a little.

Saying this, some recipes don't need oil at all, such as cooking minced beef (see page 84) – it depends on the recipe.

## Where do you put oil in the air fryer?

When cooking in an air fryer, oil goes directly onto the food. For example, when you cook chips/fries, you may imagine needing a deep pan of oil for frying. Yet in an air fryer there is no pan. Instead, you toss your chips in a tiny bit of oil in a bowl, using your hands, then tip them straight into the basket and air fry. This is amazing because it cuts down on how much oil you use, thus saving calories and saving money because a bottle of olive oil lasts a long time.

Sometimes, if you want an extra crisp to a recipe, you can simply spray a little oil directly over the food in the air fryer.

## Which oil is the best?

There are many oil options to choose from. From personal experience, value for money and crispy texture on food, we have found that extra virgin olive oil produces the best daily air fryer results.

For a treat and restaurant taste, we swap this for duck or goose fat on roast potatoes at Christmas.

## Why use an oil spray?

I am sure you have seen oil sprays being used in air fryer recipes, and we have included one in our essential air fryer accessories list (page 14). When your food is almost cooked and you just want an extra crisp on it, spray bottles are so useful for giving your food a quick spritz of oil from the top. They save your hands getting dirty and, by using a fine spray rather than a drizzle from the bottle, you are cutting down on oil usage.

## The unintentional low-fat diet

Once you get used to using so little oil, you will find yourself moving in the direction of a low-fat diet and not missing traditional fried food. When you do go out and have real fried food, such as restaurant French fries, you will likely find it greasy and a shock to your body. I know whenever Dom and I go out for dinner, we always complain that the food we once loved is really greasy. It's not, it's just the air fryer has changed our bodies for the better.

# essential air fryer accessories

It can get expensive buying numerous air fryer accessories as well as a new air fryer, so we have taken a different approach in our cookbook. We have only listed air fryer accessories that we have used in the recipes we have featured in this cookbook, and kept our list to the essentials.

**01**    **Silicone** We love silicone; it can be used again and again and easily wipes clean after use. Plus, it doesn't need greasing before use.

We recommend some **silicone cups** and **silicone round cake pans** that would fit your air fryer. You can also buy **silicone pans with handles** that work very well with deep dish meals and make it easy to get food in and out of the air fryer, like in our vegetarian lasagne on page 116.

**02**    **Ceramic** We also love to use ceramic dishes in the air fryer, such as the ramekins used for blueberry crumble (page 214) or for air frying eggs (page 31). You can use any other ceramic dishes that fit your air fryer.

**03**    **Traditional bakeware** You can also use any bakeware you would normally use in the oven that fits in your air fryer. We love individual pudding tins for Yorkshire puddings (page 173), pizza pans for a classic garlic bread or deep pan pizza (pages 185–6), or for stopping sticky food from making the air fryer dirty.

**04**    **Spray bottle** This is essential for filling with your olive oil so that you can spray it directly onto the food. Avoid oil aerosol sprays such as Pam or Fry Light because over time they will damage the air fryer.

**05**    **Thermometer** You're cooking food much faster than you're used to, and you will need to check if food is piping hot in the centre; the easiest option is to use a thermometer. The probe also doubles up as a cake tester to check cakes are set in the middle.

**06**    **Nest of bowls** These are amazing and tick so many boxes. Many sets have measuring cups for measuring ingredients, great mixing bowls, as well as sieves for when prepping ingredients. We always take them with us when we go and stay at a holiday rental with our air fryer. Or if going camping, the largest bowl can double as a washing up bowl.

**07**    It can also be handy to have **silicone spatulas** to stir your food without scratching the air fryer and a **pastry brush** for recipes that call for egg wash.

## When do you cook in bakeware?

Whilst bakeware – be it silicone, metal or ceramic – has it's place (such as using the silicone with handles for our vegetarian lasagne on page 116), we only use it when we are cooking something sticky or an item that is naturally cooked in a container, such as a cake or pie.

However, most food should be cooked directly in the air fryer basket so that fat can drain away and the air can circulate more efficiently. For example, cooking a whole chicken in a container will mean that you will end up with your chicken sitting in the fat, making it greasy, and the bakeware may also interfere with the cooking time, meaning your chicken will take much longer.

## What else can you use in the air fryer?

The short answer is that any cookware that is oven or microwave friendly is air fryer friendly. Although, it must fit in the air fryer and it can often be a challenge finding items you like that fit. More than a decade on from getting our first air fryer and we still find ourselves looking in shops for something new that will fit in the air fryer.

You can use stainless steel, ceramic, silicone or even foil trays. We love ramekins, small pizza pans, cake pans, mini loaf pans and mini pudding basins.

But mostly we use silicone because of its ability to wipe clean, and you don't need to soak it or line it with baking parchment. In fact, our first air fryer accessory was a silicone baking mat cut to size for the air fryer because no accessories were available back in 2012.

## Can you use foil in the air fryer?

Yes, you can use foil in the air fryer, but you generally only need to if the food is sticky or you need to create a tray to stop liquids escaping. For example, with our corn on the cob (page 162), we use foil to collect the melted butter to roll the corn in. Or for our chocolate chip cookies (page 209) we use a layer of foil to stop the cookies from sticking to the air fryer basket and it can also be used to easily lift the cookies from the basket.

But we don't recommend wrapping food tightly in foil regularly because it really slows down the cooking time, which defeats the purpose of the air fryer. We only do this in a handful of recipes, such as the roasted garlic on page 155 because the garlic needs to be well covered, or with meatloaf on page 83 to help keep the shape of the meat.

## Can you use baking parchment in the air fryer?

Yes, just like with foil, baking parchment can be used in the air fryer. In the Milner house, we rarely use baking parchment (or greaseproof paper or baking paper) and much prefer to use silicone because it can be reused without waste and wipes clean easily.

## Can you use paper bags in the air fryer?

We don't recommend it. We have seen the trend of cooking "chicken in a bag" where you place a whole chicken – in the special bag you buy it in – in the oven to cook. In the air fryer the brown paper bag burns and is a fire risk. The same has happened when we have done popcorn in a bag, so avoid this too.

## Can you put glass in the air fryer?

Yes, you can put glass in the air fryer, but it does slow the cook time down on a recipe by a LOT. More so than food cooked in foil. This is because with an air fryer the air is circulating all around the food, and the glass at the bottom of the container blocks the air circulation. We find that ramekins and other ceramics do a better job and we choose to use those instead.

# let's talk air fryer temperatures

**Now that we have run through our top tips, main ingredients and air fryer accessories, let's talk air fryer temperatures – which temperatures you will use the most and how to test that your air fryer is reaching the correct temperature.**

There are five main air fryer temperatures that you will need to learn:

- **75°C/165°F** Perfect for proving bread dough, defrosting food or even keeping something warm.

- **120°C/250°F** This is the temperature used for air frying eggs; any higher and the eggs will go like rubber. It is also a gentler heat that's useful for melting butter or chocolate

- **160°C/320°F** This lower temperature helps ensure that food is cooked in the centre before you raise the temperature to get it crispy on the outside.

- **180°C/360°F** This is the air fryer temperature you will use the most. Many air fryers are even pre-set to this temperature.

- **200°C/400°F** This is temperature we use to crisp stuff. Add a little extra virgin olive oil spray to the food and increase the air fryer to this temperature for 2–3 minutes and you will have crispy food.

## The problem with temperature inconsistency

Now you know your main temperatures, let's talk about the air fryer's biggest problem – not all air fryers reach the temperature they say they are. I have lost count of how many people have emailed me and said a recipe wasn't cooked enough or wasn't crispy like ours; the subject line normally starts with "What did I do wrong?"

During the recipe testing process of this cookbook, we learnt that what was 160°C/320°F in one air fryer might be 180°C/360°F in another, or even 200°C/400°F in another. You may have noticed this with standard ovens too – perhaps you hated a specific oven because it always burnt your food on top? This is the same with air fryers, and it's because of this that we created our air fryer temperature test, which is explained on the next page.

# Air fryer temperature test

We class air fryers as "slow", "average" or "fast" and we have made sure our times and temperatures on recipes throughout the cookbook match an "average" air fryer.

In our kitchen, we have three slow air fryers, three average and one fast. By adjusting the temperature accordingly, we can cook the exact food in each and it will look and taste identical. Many of our readers will tweak the recipe to suit their air fryer brand.

For example, if a recipe calls for 180°C/360°F and we are using a fast air fryer, we would cook it at 160°C/320°F; if our air fryer is slow, we would set it to 200°C/400°F. If we are using an average air fryer, we will stick to 180°C/360°F.

## The 20°C/40°F temperature rule

In a nutshell, you are moving the temperature by 20°C/40°F to accommodate the speed of your air fryer.

This rule works for all the temperatures we use for cooking the recipes in this book. For example, air fryer boiled eggs cook at 120°C/250°F and you would change this to 100°C/210°F for a fast air fryer or 140°C/280°F for a slow one.

## But which air fryer is yours?

The best way to find out is to cook some of the easiest recipes from this cookbook. Start with 180°C/360°F, then if you feel the food isn't cooked enough, try 200°C/400°F next time. If the food seems overcooked, try again at 160°C/320°F. Do this for at least five of the recommended recipes opposite to test your air fryer temperature.

If after doing the test you find that your air fryer is *not* average, you know to increase or decrease the temperature in future air fryer cooking. Pick five of these recipes to perform a temperature test on and only preheat if your air fryer automatically performs one:

- Too-Good-to-be-Frozen Chips (page 20)
- Easy-Peel Hard-Boiled Eggs (page 29)
- Air Fryer Toast (page 36)
- Uncomplicated Butternut Squash (page 148)
- Garlic Mushrooms (page 154)
- Roasted Garlic (page 155)
- Crispy Curried Chickpeas (page 124)
- Easy Cajun Potato Wedges (page 143)
- Baby Potatoes (page 137)
- Salmon Fillets (page 90)
- Whole chicken (page 46)
- Frozen chicken nuggets (page 66)

Once you have done your five, you will know how your air fryer really performs.

If a recipe calls for 200°C/400°F and you are using a slow air fryer, it will mean that you should cook the food on 220°C/430°F – but what if you have hit the temperature limit? In situations like this, we usually either add 5 minutes to the cook time at 200°C/400°F, or we start the recipe with an 8-minute preheat.

It's all about getting to know your air fryer and what its cooking heat is really like – have fun trying new recipes as you experiment.

# let's begin with frozen

Now we have explained a few air fryer beginner steps to you, let's get started by cooking frozen foods in the air fryer.

Frozen food is the ideal starting point after getting the air fryer out of its box as you get to see how air technology works, and how good your air fryer is at crisping food. You can also get a quick lesson in understanding your air fryer buttons before you move on to other great air fryer recipes.

Go shopping and buy your favourite frozen food. We chose frozen chips/fries, fish and chips, chicken wings and mozzarella sticks.

The general rule with air fryer frozen food is that if you would normally oven bake the food, you don't need extra oil; if you would normally deep fry it, then a little spray of extra virgin olive oil can make it super crispy in the air fryer.

You can also cook from frozen anything you would cook frozen in the oven, deep fat fryer, or the grill/broiler.

Keep an eye out for frozen instructions. In many of the recipes in the book we have added frozen times and temperatures.

# air fryer frozen food (four ways)

After following these four great ways to cook frozen food, you will realise how simple air frying is and how cooking times and temperatures may vary, but the principle stays the same.

## too-good-to-be-frozen chips

Whether you call them chips, fries or frites, they make the best starting point and you get to see how crispy you can make potatoes in your air fryer.

SERVES **4**
PREP **1 MINUTE**
COOK TIME **20 MINUTES**
CALORIES **436**

900g/2lb frozen chips/fries
Extra virgin olive oil spray
Salt and black pepper

**01** Place frozen chips in the air fryer basket, spreading them out so that they cook evenly. Cook at 180ºC/360ºF for 12 minutes.

**02** When the air fryer beeps, shake the chips and spray the tops with extra virgin olive oil. Air fry at 200ºC/400ºF for a further 8 minutes, or until nice and crispy.

**03** Season with salt and pepper, and serve.

You will love the simplicity of air fryer frozen wings. Perfect for game day, or a Saturday night supper. Even better, leave the wings in the air fryer for up to 45 minutes and they will stay warm.

900g/2lb frozen chicken wings
About 3 tbsp of your favourite sauce, such as buffalo or ranch (optional)

# game night frozen wings

SERVES **4**   PREP **2 MINUTES**   COOK TIME **20 MINUTES**   CALORIES **373**

**01** Place your favourite frozen chicken wings into the air fryer basket, spreading them out so that they cook evenly.

**02** Air fry the chicken wings at 180ºC/360ºF for 20 minutes, or until the chicken reaches an internal temperature of 70ºC/160ºF or above, then toss in enough of your favourite sauce to coat them, if wished. If cooking small chicken wings, reduce the cook time to just 15 minutes.

**Got a frozen sauce with your wings?** Load the frozen plastic packet into the air fryer for the last 4 minutes of the cooking time. It will defrost and warm through with the wings. Then when the wings are cooked, place them in a bowl, pour the sauce over and toss with tongs.

For a simple party food to air fry, it doesn't get any better than cheese sticks. They are also easy to pair with other party food and cook together in the air fryer.

12 frozen mozzarella sticks

# crispy mozzarella sticks

SERVES **2**   PREP **1 MINUTE**   COOK TIME **8 MINUTES**   CALORIES **281**

**01** Place the frozen mozzarella sticks in the air fryer basket, spreading them out so that they cook evenly.

**02** Air fry at 180ºC/360ºF for 8 minutes, or until crispy.

**Similar cooking times** Check out the frozen food cooking chart on pages 24–5 and look for other food with an 8-minute cook time to cook with the mozzarella sticks.

# friday night battered fish & chips

This is when you learn the skill of balancing times when air fryer cooking, which can then be used for making many air fryer dinners.

When you have two items to cook which have different cooking times, we recommend starting with the longer cook time and then adding the other item later. This will mean all your food is piping hot when served.

..............................................

SERVES **2**
PREP **2 MINUTES**
COOK TIME **30 MINUTES**
CALORIES **762**

..............................................

2 beer-battered frozen fish
   fillets
450g/1lb frozen thick cut
   chips/fries
Salt and vinegar

**01** Place the frozen chips into the air fryer basket, spreading them out so that they cook evenly. Cook at 180ºC/360ºF for 15 minutes.

**02** When the air fryer beeps, add the fish fillets over the chips. Air fry at the same temperature for a further 15 minutes, or until the fish is reading an internal temperature of 70ºC/160ºF or above and the fish fillets and chips are crispy.

**03** Season with salt and vinegar, and serve.

**Beer-battered is the best!** You can use either beer-battered or breaded fish. We find beer-battered frozen fish tastes like it's from an English chippy, and would recommend this over breaded.

# air fryer frozen cook times chart

| food name | °C/°f | time | notes |
| --- | --- | --- | --- |
| Cauliflower bites | 180°C/360°F | 6 minutes | |
| Halloumi fries | 180°C/360°F | 8 minutes | (spray with oil) |
| Onion rings | 200°C/400°F | 10 minutes | (spray with oil) |
| Boneless wings | 180°C/360°F | 14 minutes | (spray with oil) |
| Party sausage rolls | 180°C/360°F | 12 minutes | (egg wash) |
| Breaded mushrooms | 180°C/360°F | 10 minutes | |
| Sweet-and-sour chicken balls | 180°C/360°F | 12 minutes | (spray with oil) |
| Spring rolls | 180°C/360°F | 8 minutes | |
| Onion bhajis | 180°C/360°F | 6 minutes | (spray with oil) |
| Samosas | 180°C/360°F | 6 minutes | (spray with oil) |
| Mini pizzas | 160°C/320°F | 6 minutes | |
| Chicken strips | 180°C/360°F | 12 minutes | (spray with oil) |
| Popcorn chicken | 180°C/360°F | 8 minutes | |
| Chicken fingers | 180°C/360°F | 10 minutes | |
| Chicken Kiev | 180°C/360°F | 20 minutes | |
| Chicken pie | 180°C/360°F | 20 minutes | |
| Quarter pounder | 180°C/360°F | 15 minutes | |
| Veggie burgers | 180°C/360°F | 10 minutes | |
| Swedish meatballs | 180°C/360°F | 8 minutes | |

| | | | |
|---|---|---|---|
| **Fish fingers/sticks** | 180°C/360°F | 12 minutes | |
| **Frozen egg rolls** | 160°C/320°F | 15 minutes | (egg wash) |
| **Potato waffles** | 180°C/360°F | 8 minutes | |
| **Roast potatoes** | 180°C/360°F | 18 minutes | |
| **Potato wedges** | 180°C/360°F | 16 minutes | |
| **Potato skins** | 180°C/360°F | 10 minutes | |
| **Baked potatoes** | 160°C/320°F | 27 minutes | |
| **Curly fries** | 180°C/360°F | 15 minutes | (spray with oil) |
| **Skin-on fries** | 180°C/360°F | 20 minutes | (spray with oil) |
| **Frozen cookies** | 160°C/320°F | 8 minutes | |

# reheating food in the air fryer

As kids, we always reheated food in the microwave – especially last night's pizza. It was the best thing about a takeaway. But it was always soggy – not that we cared as kids! Reheat your food in the air fryer instead and the food is crispy and flavoursome again and the pizza will make you want to order extra just to reheat.

But before you dive in and reheat the contents of your takeaway box, there is an important temperature to consider – 160°C/320°F is the ideal reheat temperature. Don't go higher or you will be cooking the food again rather than reheating.

To reheat, place leftovers into the air fryer (on foil if sticky or saucy) and air fry for the recommended cook time in the chart below.

Let me demonstrate with some leftover pizza. Place leftover pizza slices into the air fryer basket, side by side. Air fry at 160°C/320°F for 4 minutes, or until hot, before serving.

## Reheating times

**Steak** 160°C/320°F – 6 minutes

**Chips/Fries** 180°C/360°F – 6 minutes (spray with oil)

**Fish and chips** 160°C/320°F – 8 minutes (spray with oil)

**Quarter pounder** 160°C/320°F – 8 minutes

**Onion rings** 160°C/320°F – 6 minutes (spray with oil)

**Doner meat** 160°C/320°F – 3 minutes

**Egg rolls** 180°C/360°F – 8 minutes

**Sliced roast beef** 160°C/320°F – 3 minutes

**Quiche** 160°C/320°F – 6 minutes

**Rotisserie chicken** 160°C/320°F – 30 minutes

**Chicken wings** 180°C/360°F – 8 minutes (spray with oil)

**Apple strudel** 160°C/320°F – 5 minutes

**Whole apple pie** 160°C/320°F – 8 minutes

# BREAKFAST
# & BRUNCH

# let's start with eggs

We recommend your air-fried breakfast starts with eggs. You can begin with a soft- or hard-boiled egg, then progress to scrambled before making your first fried egg.

## soft-boiled eggs & soldiers

Here in the UK, we love our dippy eggs for breakfast on a weekend. Toast sticks, known as soldiers, dunked into soft boiled eggs make a fantastic air fryer learning curve, and you can cook both the toast and the soft dippy eggs in the air fryer.

SERVES **2**
PREP **3 MINUTES**
COOK TIME **16 MINUTES**
CALORIES **350**

....................................................

4 large eggs
2 slices Air Fryer Toast (see page 36)
Butter, for spreading

**01** Place your eggs into the air fryer basket.

**02** Air fry the eggs at 120°C/250°F for 11 minutes.

**03** When the air fryer beeps, transfer the eggs to your egg cups.

**04** Cook your toast in the air fryer, according to the recipe on page 36, then butter it and slice it widthways into soldiers about 2cm/¾in wide.

**05** Serve your boiled eggs with the toast soldiers/toast sticks for dipping into the runny yolks.

# easy-peel hard-boiled eggs

We have not boiled an egg in a pan for many years now. We love the precise time and temperature the air fryer gives, and how amazingly easy air fried eggs are to peel.

MAKES **6**
PREP **5 MINUTES**
COOK TIME **16 MINUTES**
CALORIES **83**

6 large eggs

**01** Place your eggs into the air fryer basket.

**02** Air fry the eggs at 120ºC/250ºF for 16 minutes.

**03** Let your eggs cool in a bowl of cold water for a couple of minutes, or until they are cool enough to handle.

**04** To peel, gently tap the top and bottom of the egg on a hard surface, then gently roll the egg across the surface, which will cause the shell to crack. The shell should now easily peel away.

**05** Rinse the egg, then repeat until all the eggs are peeled.

**Devilled eggs** Transform your hard boiled eggs into devilled eggs for your next party.

Slice your eggs in half, remove the yolks and put them into a bowl. Add **1 teaspoon mustard powder** and **3 tablespoons mayonnaise** to the bowl with the yolks. Season with **salt and pepper** and mix well with a fork, until the yolks are mashed into the mayo. Spoon the mixture back into the holes in the egg whites and sprinkle with **chopped fresh chives**.

**Tip** The biggest mistake making boiled eggs in the air fryer is using the wrong temperature. Many newbies to the air fryer have reported yellow, rubbery eggs. Each time I have asked for their time and temperature, it's been much higher than recommended.

Scrambled eggs are brilliant in the air fryer. Make them with two eggs (like Dom does for his breakfast) and serve them over toast with cherry tomatoes for a simple weekday breakfast.

SERVES **1**
PREP **2 MINUTES**
COOK TIME **8 MINUTES**
CALORIES **425**

Extra virgin olive oil spray
2 large eggs
1 tsp salted butter
A short vine of cherry tomatoes
Salt and black pepper
1 slice Air Fryer Toast (see page 36), to serve

# simple scrambled eggs for one

**01** Spray a small ceramic dish with olive oil and rub the oil up the sides with your fingers to stop the egg sticking.

**02** Crack your eggs into the dish and beat well with a fork. Season with salt and pepper.

**03** Place the butter in the middle of the beaten eggs, then place the dish into the air fryer basket. If serving with cherry tomatoes, add them to the air fryer too.

**04** Air fry at 180°C/360°F for 3 minutes. When the air fryer beeps, use the fork to mix the eggs. The butter will now be melted into the scrambled eggs.

**05** Cook for a further 5 minutes at the same temperature until almost set, then stir one last time before serving on toast with the tomatoes.

As a teen, I hated the idea of frying eggs; I didn't like the thought of being splashed with hot oil, as well as having to hang around the frying pan waiting for them to be done. Fried eggs in the air fryer, however, are simple and require no babysitting. Just load them into the basket and let the air fryer work its magic. You can cook just one or multiple fried eggs at once.

SERVES **2**
PREP **2 MINUTES**
COOK TIME **8 MINUTES**
CALORIES **87**

Extra virgin olive oil spray
2 large eggs
Salt and black pepper

# easiest ever fried eggs

**01** Spray two small ceramic dishes or ramekins with oil, then use your fingers to rub it around to fully grease the dishes.

**02** Crack an egg into the centre of each dish, making sure the egg yolks don't break, and season well with salt and pepper. Load the ramekins into the air fryer basket.

**03** Air fry the eggs at 180°C/360°F for 8 minutes, or until the white is fully set. Use a spatula to carefully remove the eggs from the dishes and serve warm.

# veggie-loaded egg cups

When the world started going crazy for keto, we remember most the egg cup trend. We thought they would be amazing prepared in the air fryer and we were right. They are now our breakfast staple, plus they double up for a healthy snack to take travelling or even for summer picnics in the park. They are a great way to use up any odds and ends of quick-cooking veg lurking at the back of your fridge – or try them with cheese and ham, leftover cooked veg, or anything else you would add to an omelette.

......................................

MAKES **6**
PREP **6 MINUTES**
COOK TIME **15 MINUTES**
CALORIES **48**

......................................

115g/4oz fresh vegetables
  (such as red or yellow (bell)
  peppers, mushrooms or
  spinach)
3 large eggs
1 tbsp whole/full-fat milk
1 tsp dried oregano
Salt and black pepper

**01** Chop up the veggies into small similar-sized chunks, then divide them equally among six silicone egg cups and spread out over the bases.

**02** Crack the eggs into a bowl or mixing jug and beat with a fork. Stir in the milk and oregano, and season with salt and pepper.

**03** Pour the egg mixture carefully over the vegetables until the cups are 80 per cent full.

**04** Place the egg cups carefully into the air fryer basket and air fry at 180°C/360°F for 15 minutes, or until the egg cups are fully set. Serve warm or cold.

# kitchen sink frittata

I'm not big on meal prep, but on a Sunday I always make a "kitchen sink" frittata to clear out any leftover veggies from the week. As I make it, Dom will stand behind me reminding me to add plenty of cheese. We will then reheat it in the air fryer for a fast, school-morning breakfast.

.......................................

SERVES **6**
PREP **10 MINS**
COOK TIME **47 MINS**
CALORIES **273**

.......................................

1 green (bell) pepper/capsicum
1 red (bell) pepper/capsicum
medium sweet potato (peeled and cubed)
3 medium carrots (peeled and sliced)
225g/8oz (prepared weight) peeled and diced butternut squash
1 tbsp dried parsley
1 tbsp dried chives
1 tbsp extra virgin olive oil
125g/4½oz/1½ cups grated mature/sharp Cheddar cheese
5 large eggs
180ml/6fl oz/¾ cup whole/full-fat milk
Salt and black pepper

**01** Halve, deseed and dice the peppers. Peel and dice the sweet potato, and peel and slice the carrots. Put them all in a bowl with the squash cubes and add the dried herbs and olive oil. Season with salt and pepper and mix well with your hands.

**02** Tip the vegetables into the air fryer basket and spread out. Cook at 180ºC/360ºF for 20 minutes, or until they are fork tender and starting to crisp.

**03** Transfer the veggies to a silicone baking pan and sprinkle them with the grated cheese.

**04** Using a fork, beat the eggs and milk together in a jug. Season with salt and pepper, then pour the mixture over the vegetables in the silicone pan.

**05** Place the pan in the air fryer and air fry at the same temperature for 15 minutes. Decrease the heat to 170ºC/340ºF and cook for another 7 minutes.

**06** Remove the silicone pan from the air fryer and invert a plate over the top. Carefully flip the plate and pan over together so that the frittata is turned out onto the plate. Slide the frittata back into the pan so that the bottom is now on top, then air fry at 180ºC/360ºF for a final 5 minutes, or until a thermometer inserted into the frittata comes out clean.

**Mix it up** Speed up the cooking process by using leftover cooked veggies. Or you can make this frittata after your Sunday roast – load it up with your leftovers and cook it as you finish the washing up.

# stuffed pepper breakfast omelette

Love stuffed peppers and want a filling, healthy breakfast? Then let us introduce you to breakfast stuffed peppers. These peppers are so easy and taste so good you will want to make extra to reheat in the air fryer.

......................................

SERVES **2**
PREP **5 MINS**
COOK TIME **27 MINS**
CALORIES **514**

......................................

4 red (bell) peppers/capsicums
4 large eggs
1 tbsp whole/full-fat milk
1 spring onion/scallion
125g/4½oz/1½ cups grated
  Cheddar cheese
Salt and black pepper

**01** Slice the tops off the peppers and pull out the seeds. If any are left, remove them with a teaspoon, but make sure you don't make any holes in the bottoms of the peppers.

**02** Place the peppers into the air fryer and cook at 180ºC/360ºF for 8 minutes.

**03** In the meantime, crack the eggs into a mixing jug and beat well with a fork. Add the milk, season with salt and pepper and mix.

**04** Finely slice the spring onion.

**05** When the air fryer beeps, remove any liquid from the bottom of the peppers. Divide the cheese equally among the peppers, then pour in the egg mixture and sprinkle the spring onion on the tops.

**06** Air fry the peppers at the same temperature for another 19 minutes, or until the peppers have a chargrilled look and the eggs are fully set.

# air fryer toast

The air fryer does an amazing job of replacing the toaster and any of your favourites that you would place in the toaster – sliced bread, bagels, English muffins, Pop Tarts, and so on – can be easily done in your air fryer.

Whilst I love crumpets the most and have to fight the kids for the last one, Dom prefers some thick white toasted bread with soft English butter.

......................................

SERVES **1**
PREP **2 MINS**
COOK TIME **5 MINS**
CALORIES **368**

......................................

2 slices of bread
Extra virgin olive oil spray
Butter, softened, for spreading
Your favourite toast toppings,
  such as marmalade, cream
  cheese, jam/jelly, etc
  (optional)

**01** Preheat the air fryer to 200°C/400°F for 2 minutes.

**02** Spray the top of the two slices of bread with extra virgin olive oil and place them into the air fryer basket.

**03** Air fry for 3 minutes, then flip the slices over, spray the other sides and air fry for a final 2 minutes, or longer if you want your toast crispier.

**04** Spread the slices with butter and any of your favourite toppings. This is when we have a clear out and add marmalade, cream cheese, or other items that need using up.

# buttery crumpets

SERVES **1**
PREP **2 MINS**
COOK TIME **5 MINS**
CALORIES **287**

...............................................

2 crumpets
2 tsp butter, softened

**01** Place the crumpets into the air fryer basket, making sure they are not stacked.

**02** Air fry the crumpets at 180ºC/360ºF for 2 minutes.

**03** When the air fryer beeps, spread a teaspoon of butter over the centre of each crumpet, then air fry for a further 3 minutes at the higher temperature of 200ºC/400ºF, or until toasted to your liking.

# cream cheese bagels

SERVES **1**
PREP **2 MINS**
COOK TIME **4 MINS**
CALORIES **377**

...............................................

1 bagel
1 tsp butter, softened
2 tsp cream cheese

**01** Slice the bagel in half horizontally, if needed (it may already be sliced).

**02** Spread butter on the cut sides of the bagel halves and place into the air fryer.

**03** Air fry the bagel at 200ºC/400ºF for 4 minutes, or until crispy like toast.

**04** Spread each bagel half with cream cheese before serving.

**Pop Tarts** Do you eat Pop Tarts? We loved them as kids and in the air fryer they take just 3 minutes at 200ºC/400ºF.

# full english breakfast

In the UK we love a full English breakfast – fried egg, sausages, bacon, and the option to mix and match with other breakfast staples. But all the pots and pans can be hard work. That is when an air fryer English breakfast is perfect for cooking fast, in one air fryer basket and easy to mix it up with your favourite ingredients.

........................................

SERVES **2**
PREP **5 MINS**
COOK TIME **19 MINS**
CALORIES **926**

........................................

4 thick Cumberland sausages
4 rashers/slices back bacon
2 black pudding slices
½ x 400g/14oz can baked
  beans
Extra virgin olive oil spray
2 large eggs
8 large button mushrooms
Salt and black pepper
Air Fryer Toast (see page 36),
  to serve

**01** Place the sausages and bacon rashers into the air fryer basket. If your basket is small, place the bacon under the sausages.

**02** Find a place for the black pudding and a spare area for a ramekin. Pour the baked beans into the ramekin.

**03** Set the air fryer to 180ºC/360ºF and cook for 12 minutes, or until the baked beans are bubbling and the black pudding slices are piping hot. Remove the baked beans ramekin and the black pudding and place on a plate.

**04** Spray two ramekins with olive oil, crack an egg into each and season with salt and pepper. Place them into the air fryer basket, in the spaces created by removing the beans and black pudding.

**05** Cut your mushrooms in half and place in any spare gaps in the basket. Spray the mushrooms with olive oil and season with salt and pepper.

**06** Air fry at the same temperature for a further 7 minutes, or until the sausages are brown and the bacon is crispy.

**07** Serve the English breakfast with air fryer toast.

**Tip** If you want to change any of the elements in your English breakfast, see overleaf for a list of cooking times and temperatures for popular breakfast additions.

# sausages

You can swap Cumberland sausages for any favourite sausage, including vegetarian, vegan, low fat or, our personal favourite, chicken sausages. But note that some of them may not brown as well as Cumberland sausages.

# bacon

Here in the UK, we often use back bacon which comes in slices double the size of American streaky bacon and is much leaner. We find back bacon will need 25 per cent longer to cook, especially if you want it really crispy.

# mix and match

Because many English breakfast staples require a similar cooking time and temperature, it's easy to mix and match ingredients. Swap black pudding for hash browns, fried eggs for scrambled eggs, or mushrooms for grilled tomatoes. See our list of cooking times (right) for some suggestions.

# breakfast staples times and temperatures

**Sausages** 180ºC/360ºF – 12 minutes

**Back bacon** 180ºC/360ºF – 8 minutes

**Streaky bacon** 180ºC/360ºF – 6 minutes

**Black pudding** 180ºC/360ºF – 8 minutes

**Grilled tomatoes** 180ºC/360ºF – 8 minutes

**Baked beans** (cook in a ramekin) 180ºC/360ºF – 6 minutes

**Frozen hash browns** 180ºC/360ºF – 10 minutes

**Frozen bacon** 100ºC/210ºF – 8 minutes, or until defrosted, plus 6 minutes at 200ºC/400ºF

**Frozen sausages** 160ºC/320ºF – 15 minutes

**Frozen sausage patties** 160ºC/320ºF – 12 minutes

**Frozen pancakes** 160ºC/320ºF – 6 minutes

**Frozen breakfast potatoes** 180ºC/360ºF – 15 minutes

**Frozen croissants** 180ºC/360ºF – 9 minutes

**Frozen pain au chocolat** (egg wash it first) 160ºC/320ºF – 10 minutes

# berrylicious baked oats

These baked oats are delicious – they have a banana muffin crust and a porridge/oatmeal centre. And they are so simple to make; dump the ingredients into a blender, then pour into ramekins and air fry. Perfect for a healthy air fryer breakfast.

..........................................

MAKES **4**
PREP **10 MINS**
COOK TIME **12 MINS**
CALORIES **257**

..........................................

2 medium bananas
2 large eggs
115g/4oz/1¼ cups rolled oats
80ml/2½fl oz/⅓ cup whole/
   full-fat milk
1 tbsp vanilla extract
3 tbsp Greek yoghurt, plus
   extra to serve
28g/1oz mixed berries
   (blueberries, raspberries,
   strawberries)
Extra virgin olive oil spray
Clear honey, to serve

**01** Peel the bananas, break them in half and put into a blender or food processor. Crack in the eggs, then add the oats, milk, vanilla and Greek yoghurt.

**02** Pulse the blender until you have a smooth and creamy mixture. Add the berries and pulse again for a couple of seconds.

**03** Grease four ramekins with the olive oil spray, then pour in the oat mixture, dividing it evenly among the ramekins.

**04** Place the ramekins into the air fryer basket and air fry at 180°C/360°F for 12 minutes, or until they're crusty on top and you have porridge-style centres.

**05** Serve the ramekins with extra Greek yoghurt spooned on top and a little drizzle of honey.

**Got leftover mixture?** Pour it into silicone muffin cups until they are three-quarters full, then air fry for the same time and at the same temperature. The result is banana oatmeal muffins that are perfect for taking to work or school as a mid-morning snack.

**Go bananas for banana souffle** Plan B is to make super easy souffles with a simplified version of this recipe! Add **2 large bananas**, **2 large eggs** and **1 tablespoon vanilla extract** to the blender. After pulsing together, divide among greased ramekins and air fry at 180°C/360°F for 15 minutes. They will rise like souffles and taste delicious.

# rainbow brunch bowl

This is the brunch we turn to when we want something healthy but are bored of eggs and just want to dump the ingredients into the air fryer. It's easy to mix and match with different veggies and it tastes amazing with the addition of sausages.

.............................................

SERVES **2**
PREP **10 MINS**
COOK TIME **25 MINS**
CALORIES **527**

.............................................

1 medium courgette/zucchini
1 red (bell) pepper/capsicum
225g/8oz (prepared weight) peeled and diced sweet potato
225g/8oz (prepared weight) peeled and diced butternut squash
2 tsp dried parsley
2 tsp dried mixed herbs/Italian seasoning
2 tsp sweet paprika
1 tbsp extra virgin olive oil
5 Cumberland pork sausages
Salt and black pepper

**01** Slice the courgette into thick slices, then quarter each slice. Deseed and dice the red pepper. Put them in a bowl with the sweet potato and butternut squash cubes.

**02** Add your dried herbs, paprika and the olive oil, then season with salt and pepper and mix well with your hands.

**03** Load your veggies into the air fryer basket and cook at 160ºC/320ºF for 12 minutes. Stir with a silicone spatula, then slice your sausages into quarters and place them over the veggies.

**04** Air fry at 180ºC/360ºF for a further 8 minutes, then stir the sausages into the veggies. Air fry at 200ºC/400ºF for a final 5 minutes, or until the sausages are well browned.

**05** Divide the mixture between two bowls and serve.

**Meat-free swap** Make this brunch bowl meat-free by swapping regular Cumberland sausages for vegetarian or vegan sausages.

# CHICKEN

# let's air fry a whole chicken

After seven years with our medium-sized air fryer, we upgraded to an extra-large one just to be able to cook a whole chicken. We stood in front of the air fryer with excitement when it beeped. We were amazed at how crispy our whole chicken was, without putting butter under the skin and just using a small quantity of olive oil. We have not cooked roast chicken in the oven since.

If there is an air fryer recipe you must make, then a whole chicken is it.

Even better, you learn the basic technique and then rinse and repeat with different seasonings, adding in sides or even stuffing your chicken. But first let us show you the basics.

SERVES **4**
PREP **5 MINUTES**
COOK TIME **45 MINUTES**
CALORIES **455**

1 medium whole chicken (giblets removed)
½ tbsp extra virgin olive oil
1½ tsp dried mixed herbs/Italian seasoning
Salt and black pepper

**01** Tie the chicken legs together with string.

**02** Place the whole chicken, breast side down, on a chopping board. Rub half the olive oil into all the visible skin, then sprinkle half the mixed herbs over the chicken and season with salt and pepper.

**03** Place the chicken into the air fry basket, still breast side down, and air fry at 180°C/360°F for 25 minutes.

**04** Place a fork in the cavity and use it to flip the chicken over so that it is breast side up. Drizzle with the remaining olive oil and rub into the skin, then add the remaining herbs and extra salt and pepper.

**05** Cook at the same temperature for a further 20 minutes, or until a thermometer reads an internal temperature of 70°C/160°F or above.

## Top Tips

**Choose a medium chicken** Most air fryers will only fit a medium chicken. When shopping, look for a medium or small chicken.

**Universal cook time** On average, the cook time for a whole chicken in an air fryer will be half the recommended oven-cook time on the chicken packaging.

**Reheating a whole chicken** Do you have a cooked chicken that needs to be reheated? Place your whole chicken in the air fryer basket, breast side up, and air fry at 180°C/360°F for 30 minutes.

**Season your roast chicken** Don't just follow our advice – experiment:
- Swap the mixed herbs/Italian seasoning for any other favourite dried herb.
- Go Cajun and add 1½ teaspoons of Cajun seasoning.
- Go Indian, and add ½ teaspoon each of ground cumin, garam masala and mild curry powder.
- Go Portuguese and add 1½ teaspoons of piri piri dry rub.

# roast chicken & stuffing

Beyond air frying a whole chicken as it is, you can also stuff the carcass with delicious homemade stuffing. Or make stuffing balls and cook the stuffing balls at the same time as the roast chicken. Either method creates a delicious roast chicken and stuffing recipe that is perfect for Sunday dinner.

................................................

SERVES **4**
PREP **15 MINUTES**
COOK TIME **1 HOUR**
CALORIES **616**

................................................

1 medium whole chicken
  (giblets removed)
½ tbsp extra virgin olive oil
1 tsp dried thyme
1 tsp dried parsley
Salt and black pepper

**FOR THE STUFFING**
½ medium onion
150g/5½oz sausage meat
1 tsp dried thyme
1 tsp dried parsley
1 large egg
1 heaped tbsp fresh
  breadcrumbs
Salt and black pepper

**01** To make the stuffing, finely dice the onion and put it in a mixing bowl. Add the sausage meat and dried herbs to the bowl and season with salt and pepper. Mix with your hands, breaking up any bigger bits of sausage meat as you go and making sure the ingredients are well mixed. Crack the egg into the bowl and mix, then add the breadcrumbs and mix until you have a big ball of stuffing.

**02** Put the stuffing into the chicken cavity, pushing it down to fit it all in. Once stuffed, tie up the chicken legs with string.

**03** Place the whole chicken, breast side down, into the air fryer basket. Make sure it is pressed down and fits properly. Rub half the olive oil into all the visible skin, sprinkle half the dried herbs over the chicken and season with salt and pepper.

**04** Air fry the whole chicken at 180ºC/360ºF for 30 minutes.

**05** Use tongs to help you flip over the whole chicken without burning yourself to get it breast side up.

**06** Drizzle over the remaining olive oil and rub into the skin, then add the remaining herbs and season again with salt and pepper.

**07** Cook at the same temperature for a further 30–40 minutes, or until it reads an internal temperature of 70ºC/160ºF or above before serving.

**Stuffing balls** In the Milner kitchen, we prefer stuffing balls over stuffing the cavity of the whole chicken. Plus, it helps keep the cook time down. Make our stuffing above and, instead of stuffing the carcass, divide the stuffing into six equal portions and roll into balls. Eight minutes before the chicken is done, find some gaps around the chicken and add the stuffing balls. Cook for the final 8 minutes and the chicken and stuffing will then be ready at the same time.

**Last-minute frozen whole chicken?** You can also cook a whole chicken from frozen; it takes a little longer but still tastes amazing. Perfect for answering "What's for dinner?", when all you have is a freezer of frozen food.

Place the frozen whole chicken into the air fryer basket, breast side down. Air fry at 80ºC/175ºF for 20 minutes, or until almost thawed.

Then you can follow our air fryer chicken recipe on page 46 and cook until the chicken reaches an internal temperature of 70ºC/160ºC or above at the thickest part of the breast. If the chicken is a little bigger than ours, it might need another 10 minutes cook time.

# everyday chicken breasts

In the Milner house, we often have spare chicken breasts in the fridge. We won't have a real plan for them – just know we will cook them in the air fryer and they can be dinner. That's the beauty of air fryer chicken breasts; start by air frying these breasts and then you can make them into so many meals (see our tips).

................................................

SERVES **4**
PREP **2 MINUTES**
COOK TIME **18 MINUTES**
CALORIES **141**

................................................

4 medium skinless and boneless
   chicken breasts
Extra virgin olive oil spray
A couple of pinches of garlic
   powder
1 tsp dried mixed herbs/Italian
   seasoning
1 tsp dried parsley
Salt and black pepper

**01** Place the chicken breasts into the air fryer basket. Spray the top of the chicken with olive oil and sprinkle with a pinch of garlic, half the dried herbs and salt and pepper until you have an even coating.

**02** Air fry the chicken breasts at 180ºC/360ºF for 12 minutes, then turn the chicken over with tongs.

**03** Now repeat the seasoning process with another spray of oil, and the remaining garlic and herbs, seasoning again with salt and pepper.

**04** Air fry at the same temperature for a further 6 minutes, or until the chicken reads an internal temperature of 70ºC/160ºF or above.

## What to do with your chicken breasts:

- Serve them with veggies.
- Turn them into a chicken salad.
- Let them be the star of taco Tuesday.
- Use them in any recipes that call for rotisserie chicken.
- Shred the chicken and use it in wraps or for work lunches.
- Have fun with the kids and make chicken nuggets (see page 66).

**Prefer chicken thighs?** We love how flavoursome boneless chicken thighs are and often swap breasts for thigh fillets. If swapping for thighs, we recommend cooking at 180ºC/360ºF for 25 minutes.

# ultimate balsamic chicken bowl

You have made chicken breasts in the air fryer and now you would like to make them into a meal.

Balsamic chicken is just perfect and my favourite air fryer summer meal. Chicken breast is cut into chunks and air fried with lots of veggies for a summer bowl of yum.

SERVES **4**
PREP **12 MINUTES, PLUS MARINATING**
COOK TIME **22 MINUTES**
CALORIES **221**

1 red (bell) pepper/capsicum
1 orange (bell) pepper/ capsicum
1 medium courgette/zucchini
250g/9oz button mushrooms
3 medium skinless and boneless chicken breasts
12 cherry tomatoes
A handful of rocket/arugula leaves
Salt and black pepper

**FOR THE BALSAMIC MARINADE**
1 tbsp balsamic vinegar
1 tbsp clear honey
1 tbsp extra virgin olive oil
1 tsp dried basil
1 tsp dried oregano
¼ tsp garlic powder

**01** Deseed the peppers and cut them into bite-sized cubes. Slice the courgette into 6mm/¼in thick slices, then cut into quarters. Clean the mushrooms and slice them in half.

**02** Cut each chicken breast into eight bite-sized pieces, then season generously with salt and pepper.

**03** Next, add the marinade ingredients to a large bowl and mix well with a spoon. Add the chicken and veggies to the bowl and mix again with your hands for an even coating. Cover the bowl with cling film/plastic wrap and place in the fridge for 2 hours to marinate.

**04** Once marinated, tip the chicken and veggies into the air fryer basket and spread them out. Air fry at 180ºC/360ºF for 12 minutes.

**05** Add the whole cherry tomatoes to the air fryer and stir with a wooden spoon. Air fry at the same temperature for a further 10 minutes, or until the chicken reads an internal temperature of 70ºC/160ºF or above.

**06** Stir the rocket into the chicken and veg, then divide into four bowls and serve.

**Let balsamic be your air fryer hero** Balsamic vinegar is brilliant for stopping food from drying out in the air fryer. Replacing half the oil in a recipe with the same amount of balsamic is also a fantastic way of reducing your oil intake.

# cheesy chicken wrapped in parma ham

We remember being introduced to cheesy chicken wrapped in Parma ham many years ago and thinking it was the best way ever to enjoy chicken. Then we got an air fryer and it became even better! The chicken stays super moist, the Parma ham goes ultra crispy, and then you have all that yummy cheese in the centre.

......................................

SERVES **2**
PREP **8 MINUTES**
COOK TIME **25–30 MINUTES**
CALORIES **382**

......................................

2 medium chicken breasts
28g/1oz mini mozzarella balls
1½ tbsp light garlic and herb
   cream cheese
20g/⅔oz/¼ cup grated
   Parmesan cheese
6–8 slices Parma ham, as
   needed
Salt and black pepper

**01**  Season the chicken breasts with salt and pepper. With a sharp knife, slice down the middle of a chicken breast lengthways, cutting three-quarters of the way through to create a pocket inside. Repeat to cut pockets in the other chicken breast.

**02**  Cut the mini mozzarella balls into thin slices. Fill each pocket with half the cream cheese, followed by half the mozzarella and finally half the Parmesan.

**03**  Wrap the Parma ham slices tightly around each chicken breast so that the ham completely seals the cheese inside the chicken. Depending on the size of your chicken breasts, you might need a fourth slice. Repeat to stuff the second chicken breast.

**04**  Place the chicken breasts into the air fryer basket and air fry at 180ºC/360ºF for 25 minutes or 30 minutes for a larger chicken breast. When the air fryer beeps, do an internal temperature check to make sure the chicken is at 70ºC/160ºF or above before serving.

# honey garlic chicken thighs & potatoes

When we were recording recipe videos, we had 15 different air fryer recipes on the side to choose from for our lunch. It was this recipe – a reader's favourite – that won, and involved a fight over who got the last honey flavoured potato! If you want an easy air fryer chicken and potatoes recipe, this one wins every time.

SERVES **2**
PREP **15 MINUTES**
COOK TIME **35 MINUTES**
CALORIES **756**

6 medium potatoes
2 tsp extra virgin olive oil
1 tbsp dried parsley
1 tsp garlic purée
4 bone-in, skin-on chicken thighs
Salt and black pepper

**FOR THE HONEY GLAZE**
1 tsp extra virgin olive oil
1 tsp garlic purée
2 tsp dried parsley
1 tsp wholegrain mustard
1 tsp Dijon mustard
1 tbsp clear honey

**01** Scrub the potatoes and cut them into cubes, leaving the skin on. Put them in a mixing bowl with the olive oil, parsley and garlic. Season with salt and pepper and mix well with your hands so that the potatoes are evenly coated.

**02** Load the potatoes into the air fryer basket and air fry at 180ºC/360ºC for 5 minutes, to give the potatoes a head start on the chicken.

**03** When the air fryer beeps, shake the potatoes, then place the chicken thighs on top of the potatoes. Season the chicken well with salt and pepper. Air fry the chicken and potatoes together at the same temperature for 15 minutes.

**04** In the meantime, put all the ingredients for the honey glaze in a bowl (you can use the same one you used for the potatoes so you save on washing up). Mix well with a spoon.

**05** When the air fryer beeps, use a pastry brush to coat the chicken thighs with the sticky honey glaze.

**06** Air fry the chicken and potatoes at 180ºC/360ºF for a final 15 minutes, or until the chicken reaches an internal temperature of 70ºC/160ºF or above and the potatoes are nice and crispy.

# sticky barbecue chicken wings

While crispy chicken wings from the the air fryer are most associated with game day and the super bowl, we just love them for a Saturday night treat with a movie.

.....................................................

SERVES **4**
PREP **5 MINUTES, PLUS MARINATING**
COOK TIME **20 MINUTES**
CALORIES **489**

.....................................................

900g/2lb chicken wings
2 tsp extra virgin olive oil
1 heaped tsp sweet paprika
1 heaped tsp dried oregano
1 tsp dried barbecue rub/
  seasoning
A pinch of garlic powder
Salt and black pepper
4 tbsp barbecue or hot sauce,
  to serve

**01** Put the chicken wings in a large bowl and add the olive oil. Add all the herbs and spices to the bowl, season generously with salt and pepper and mix well until the wings have a lovely orange colour. Cover the bowl with cling film/plastic wrap and place in the fridge for a couple of hours to marinate.

**02** Once marinated, load the chicken wings into the air fryer basket. Air fry at 180ºC/360ºF for 15 minutes, then turn the wings with tongs and air fry at the same temperature for a final 5 minutes, or until you have crispy skin and the chicken reads an internal temperature of 70ºC/160ºF or above.

**03** Serve them with dipping sauce or toss in barbecue or hot sauce, depending on how you like your wings.

# tandoori chicken

In this tandoori chicken recipe, we are combining delicious yoghurt marinated chicken with sweet potato, squash, chickpeas, and red peppers.

SERVES **2**
PREP **10 MINUTES, PLUS MARINATING**
COOK TIME **28 MINUTES**
CALORIES **1088**

3 chicken thighs
3 chicken drumsticks
½ medium butternut squash
1 medium sweet potato
1 tsp smoked paprika
1 tsp tandoori seasoning
1 tbsp garlic purée
1 tbsp tomato purée/paste
1 tbsp extra virgin olive oil
1 red (bell) pepper/capsicum
1 × 400g/14oz can chickpeas
2 mini naan breads
Salt and black pepper

## FOR THE CHICKEN MARINADE
370g/13oz/1½ cups natural
  yoghurt
1 tbsp tomato purée/paste
1 tbsp garlic purée
2 tsp ginger purée
2 tsp lemon juice
1 tbsp garam masala
2 tsp ground cumin
1 tsp ground turmeric
1 tbsp dried coriander/cilantro
  leaf

## FOR THE DIPPING SAUCE
245g/9oz/1 cup natural yoghurt
A handful of mint leaves
½ tsp lemon juice

**01** Put all the marinade ingredients into a large bowl and mix well. Set 4 tablespoons of the marinade aside in another bowl. Season the chicken with salt and pepper, then add the chicken to the main bowl and mix to make sure the chicken is well coated with the marinade. Cover the bowl with cling film/plastic wrap and place in the fridge to marinate for 12–24 hours. Also cover the bowl with the reserved 4 tablespoons of marinade and place in the fridge.

**02** When you are ready to cook, peel and dice the butternut squash and sweet potato. Place the veg in a bowl and season with salt and pepper. Add the smoked paprika, tandoori seasoning, garlic purée, tomato purée and olive oil. Mix well with your hands until well coated.

**03** Put the butternut squash and sweet potato cubes in the air fryer basket to the left. Remove the chicken pieces from the marinade, giving them a good shake to remove any excess marinade, and place them to the right of the air fryer basket.

**04** Air fry at 180ºC/360ºF for 15 minutes. Turn the chicken over with tongs and air fry at the same temperature for another 5 minutes, or until the chicken reads an internal temperature of 70ºC/160ºF or above.

**05** Whilst the chicken is cooking, dice the red pepper into 1cm/½ inch cubes and drain and rinse the canned chickpeas. Put the peppers and chickpeas into the bowl with the reserved marinade. Mix well with your hands.

**06** When the chicken is cooked, remove it from the air fryer and allow to rest. Add the chickpeas and peppers to the space created in the air fryer basket, and give the sweet potato and butternut squash a stir with a silicone spatula. Air fry at the same temperature for a further 5 minutes.

**07** In the meantime, add all the ingredients for the mint yoghurt sauce into a food processor and blitz until the mint is finely chopped.

**08** When the air fryer beeps, give the basket a shake, then place the naan breads on top of the veggies. Cook at the same temperature for a further 3 minutes, or until the naan bread is warmed through and the butternut squash and sweet potatoes are fork tender.

**09** Place the naan bread onto two dinner plates, then cover with the veggies, followed by the chicken and finally a drizzle of your yoghurt sauce.

# air fryer breaded chicken (three ways)

We remember the first time we cooked breaded chicken in the air fryer; we made Southern fried chicken drumsticks and couldn't believe how good they tasted. The chicken was so tender and the breading was too good to be true. They tasted too good to have been cooked without any oil.

We then worked our way through every breaded food we could think of and this one technique was repeated many times.

We're going to demonstrate first, with step-by-step photos, how to air fry Southern fried chicken (see page 64 for the full recipe). Then we'll show you how to adjust the recipe for schnitzel and, the kids' favourite, chicken nuggets in the recipes that follow.

Imagine what else you can do with the same technique: chicken fingers, fish fingers, onion rings, spam fritters, fish burgers and breaded pork chops are all options. You can then advance to making our fish and chips from page 97, which combines this breading technique with chips from page 129.

## Top Tips

**Season the chicken** You can have the best flavoured breading, but it's disappointing if you then bite into the chicken and it's plain and boring. We recommend that you season the chicken first before beginning the production line.

**Make a production line** It's very important that you create a production line – a flour bowl, an egg bowl and a breadcrumbs bowl. Then it's quick and simple to bread food.

**Left and right hand** Dom recommends that you use your left hand for the flour and the egg, and your right hand for the breadcrumbs. It will stop you adding wet egg to your breadcrumbs bowl.

**Quantities** If you have breadcrumbs left, we recommend you recycle them and use in an extra breaded recipe, such as some quick nuggets or some fritters.

**Seasoning mix** We make a bulk batch of the fried chicken seasoning, then keep it in our herb cupboard ready to use next time. It also makes a delicious seasoning on other breaded foods, as well as on a whole chicken or chicken breasts.

## essential breaded chicken cooking times

**Popcorn chicken** 180ºC/360ºF – 12 minutes

**Chicken strips** 180ºC/360ºF – 12 minutes

**Chicken cordon bleu** 180ºC/360ºF – 15 minutes

**Chicken wings** 180ºC/360ºF – 20 minutes

# southern fried chicken

When we lived in Portugal, they often had a special price for chicken legs. We would bulk buy them and Dom would cut them into thighs and drumsticks. Then for dinner we would have fried chicken and corn on the cob (page 162) and some shop-bought coleslaw. So good and cheap to make too!

SERVES **2**
PREP **10 MINUTES**
COOK TIME **26 MINUTES**
CALORIES **856**

3 medium chicken legs, jointed
   to make 3 drumsticks and
   3 thighs
1½ tbsp dried poultry
   seasoning
130g/4½oz/1 cup plain
   (all-purpose) flour
2 large eggs
½ tsp garlic powder
100g/3½oz/2 cups fresh
   breadcrumbs
Salt and black pepper

**FOR THE SOUTHERN FRIED
CHICKEN SEASONING**
2 tsp smoked paprika
2 tsp dried oregano
2 tsp dried tarragon
2 tsp dried parsley
2 tsp dried chives
2 tsp dried thyme
1 tsp dried poultry seasoning
¼ tsp garlic powder
A pinch of cayenne pepper

**01** Generously season the chicken pieces with 2 teaspoons of the poultry seasoning and salt and pepper. Place on a large plate, cover and place in the fridge for an hour.

**02** Create the production line: put the flour and the remaining poultry seasoning in the first bowl and mix together. In the second bowl, combine the eggs and garlic powder, and season with salt and pepper. Beat with a fork. In the third and final bowl, combine all the ingredients for the Southern fried chicken seasoning. Add the breadcrumbs to the bowl and season generously with salt and pepper and mix well with a fork.

**03** Position the three bowls from left to right to make breading even easier, with flour left, eggs in the centre and breadcrumbs to the right.

**04** To coat the chicken pieces, dip them first in the flour bowl, turning to coat, then drench in egg and let the excess drip off. Finally, roll in the breadcrumbs until each piece is fully covered in crumbs.

**05** Place the chicken pieces into the air fryer basket, making sure they are spread out and not touching one another. If your air fryer is small, then the chicken can be cooked in batches. Air fry at 180ºC/360ºF for 26 minutes, or until a thermometer reads an internal temperature of 70ºC/160ºF or above in the thickest part and they are golden and crispy.

# homemade chicken nuggets

**Got a spare chicken breast or made breaded chicken and made too much breading? That is when chicken nuggets are perfect. One chicken breast makes eight nuggets and is perfect for easy family dinners.**

.....................................

SERVES **4**
PREP **10 MINUTES, PLUS MARINATING**
COOK TIME **10 MINUTES**
CALORIES **300**

.....................................

2 medium chicken breasts
2 tsp dried poultry seasoning
130g/4½oz/1 cup plain
  (all-purpose) flour
1 tbsp dried parsley
2 large eggs
½ tsp garlic powder
100g/3½oz/2 cups fresh
  breadcrumbs
1 tbsp dried barbecue
  seasoning
Salt and black pepper

**01** Chop the chicken breasts in half lengthways, then each half into four, so that you are left with 16 similar-sized pieces. Generously season the chicken with poultry seasoning and salt and pepper. Place on a large plate, cover and place in the fridge for an hour.

**02** Create a production line: put the flour, parsley and salt and pepper in the first bowl. In the second bowl, combine the eggs and garlic powder, and season with salt and pepper. Beat with a fork. In the third and final bowl, mix the breadcrumbs with the dried barbecue seasoning and season generously with salt and pepper.

**03** To coat the chicken nuggets, dip them first in the flour bowl, turning to coat, then drench in egg and let the excess drip off. Finally, roll in the breadcrumbs until each nugget is fully covered in crumbs.

**04** Place the chicken nuggets into the air fryer basket, making sure they are spread out and not touching one another. Air fry at 180°C/360°F for 10 minutes, or until a thermometer reads an internal temperature of 70°C/160°F or above in the thickest part and they are golden and crispy.

**Frozen chicken nuggets** You can also cook frozen chicken nuggets in the air fryer. We recommend that you air fry at 180°C/360°F for 9 minutes, or until piping hot throughout.

# super-crispy chicken schnitzel

**"Daddy, please make schnitzel like we had in Germany?"** says Sofia. She loves the crispy coating on the chicken and would have Dom bread it for her every day if he agreed. You can follow this schnitzel recipe with chicken, or swap the chicken for pork or veal.

......................................

SERVES **2**
PREP **10 MINUTES, PLUS MARINATING**
COOK TIME **12 MINUTES**
CALORIES **589**

......................................

2 medium chicken breasts
2 tsp dried mixed herbs/Italian
   seasoning
130g/4½oz/1 cup plain
   (all-purpose) flour
1 tbsp dried parsley
2 large eggs
½ tsp garlic powder
100g/3½oz/2 cups fresh
   breadcrumbs
1 tbsp dried poultry seasoning
Salt and black pepper

**01** Start by butterflying the chicken breasts to flatten them out. Place a breast on a chopping board and position a sharp knife at the side. Slice horizontally, cutting about three quarters of the way through, then open the chicken out like a book. Repeat to butterfly the second chicken breast.

**02** Generously season the chicken with the mixed herbs and salt and pepper. Place on a large plate, cover and place in the fridge for an hour.

**03** Create a production line: put the flour, parsley and salt and pepper in the first bowl. In the second bowl, combine the eggs and garlic powder, and season with salt and pepper. Beat with a fork. In the third and final bowl, mix the breadcrumbs with the dried poultry seasoning and season generously with salt and pepper.

**04** To coat the butterflied chicken breasts, dip them first in the flour bowl, turning to coat, then drench in egg and let the excess drip off. Finally, roll in the breadcrumbs until each piece is fully covered in crumbs.

**05** Place the chicken schnitzel into the air fryer basket, making sure they are not touching one another. If your air fryer is small, you might need to cook them in two batches. Air fry at 180ºC/360ºF for 12 minutes, or until a thermometer reads 70ºC/160ºF or above in the thickest part and they are golden and crispy.

**Frozen chicken schnitzel** You can also cook frozen chicken schitzel in the air fryer. We recommend you air fry at 180ºC/360ºF for 8 minutes, then turn them over with tongs and cook for a final 8 minutes at 160ºC/320ºF until golden and piping hot throughout.

# MEAT

# let's air fry steak

There is no going back to the grill/broiler or the frying pan once you have cooked steak in the air fryer.

The first time Dom and I tried it, we used sirloin. We had it with skin-on fries and sat at the table speechless. We were lost for words because it was so good and so easy.

Any steak you would pan fry or barbecue can be air fried. Some of our favourite steaks to air fry include sirloin, New York strip, fillet, filet mignon, ribeye, T-bone, flank, skirt and rump.

# how to cook steaks in the air fryer

The technique of cooking steak in the air fryer is a very simple one. Steak, regardless of type, is cooked for equal time on each side.

You season it with your favourite seasonings, cook, flip, cook again and, after letting it rest for a couple of minutes, it is done. Then you can repeat, mixing your steak up with other ingredients – serve steak with chips, or try making a simple surf and turf.

2 × 225g/8oz sirloin/New York
   strip steaks
1 tsp garlic powder
Salt and black pepper

SERVES **2**
PREP **2 MINUTES**
COOK TIME **10 MINUTES**
CALORIES **456**

**01** Place the two sirloin steaks side by side in the air fryer basket. Season with salt and pepper and sprinkle half the garlic powder over the two steaks.

**02** Air fry the steaks at 180ºC/360ºF for 5 minutes, then turn the steaks over using tongs. Season again with salt, pepper and the remaining garlic powder and air fry at the same temperature for a further 5 minutes.

**03** Allow the steak to rest for a couple of minutes before serving.

## Reheating Steak

I don't know about you, but when we eat out at a steak restaurant, we get way too much. We recommend you bring your leftovers home and reheat the steak in the air fryer. To do this, place it in the air fryer and air fry at 160ºC/320ºF for 6 minutes.

## Cooking Steak from Frozen

You can also cook steak from frozen. Season as above and air fry at 160ºC/320ºF for 13 minutes, then turn the steak over with tongs and air fry at 180ºC/360ºF for a final 5 minutes.

## Go Surf and Turf

Another option is to add some prawns/shrimp and turn it into a surf and turf.

We have found the best option is frozen raw peeled king prawns, or as they are called across the globe, peeled shrimp. They cook really well in the air fryer and are also great value for money.

Cook the steak and the prawns in the air fryer together, following our steak recipe opposite. When you go to flip the steak over, shake the prawns, and when you serve your surf and turf, add a squeeze of lemon juice to the prawns.

## Steak Cuts Cooking Times

**Rump** 180ºC/360ºF – 6 minutes each side
**T-bone** 180ºC/360ºF – 9 minutes each side
**Fillet** 180ºC/360ºF – 4 minutes each side
**Ribeye** 180ºC/360ºF – 5 minutes each side
**Skirt** 160ºC/320ºF – 9 minutes each side
**Flank** 160ºC/320ºF – 9 minutes each side

These cook times work for a steak cooked to 'medium'. Add 2 more minutes each side for medium–well done, or 3 minutes each side for well done.

# steak & chips

**Steak and chips is one of Dom's and my favourite dinners. We would often have *steak frites* (the French name) when eating out in France or Belgium and it comes together so easily in the air fryer.**

SERVES **2**
PREP **8 MINUTES**
COOK TIME **20 MINUTES**
CALORIES **712**

4 medium white potatoes
1 tbsp extra virgin olive oil
2 tsp dried parsley
2 × 175g/6oz fillet steaks/filet mignon
1 tsp steak seasoning
1 tsp garlic powder
2 tsp garlic butter (optional)
Salt and black pepper

**01** Peel the potatoes and slice them into chips/fries. Aim for a universal size so that they cook evenly.

**02** Put the chips into a mixing bowl and add the olive oil and parsley, and season with salt and pepper. Mix the ingredients well with your hands so that the chips are evenly coated.

**03** Load the chips into the air fryer basket and spread out. Air fry at 180ºC/360ºF for 12 minutes, or until fork tender.

**04** Give the chips a shake, then add the fillet steaks over the chips. Sprinkle half the steak seasoning and garlic powder over them and generously season with salt and pepper. Air fry at the same temperature for a further 4 minutes.

**05** Turn the steaks over using tongs, season again with the remaining steak seasoning and garlic powder, and salt and pepper, then cook for a final 4 minutes. If you want to add garlic butter, place a teaspoon of it on each steak 1 minute before the end of the cooking time and it will melt as the steak finishes cooking.

# saturday night fruity pork steaks

Back when Kyle was a toddler, Dom and I would have pork steaks as our weekly treat for supper on a Saturday night. With Kyle tucked up in bed, we could sit down to enjoy what we thought was the best dinner ever. Now we've converted the recipe for the air fryer and it's even better. We love to pair these pork steaks with homemade chips (see page 129).

......................................

SERVES **2**
PREP **10 MINUTES**
COOK TIME **14 MINUTES**
CALORIES **479**

......................................

2 red apples
2 pears
Extra virgin olive oil spray
1 tsp ground cinnamon
2 × 225g/8oz pork steaks
2 tsp pork or poultry
   seasoning/rub
Salt and black pepper

**01** Leaving the skins on, dice the apples and pears. Place them into the air fryer basket, spreading them out. Spray with olive oil and sprinkle with cinnamon.

**02** Place the pork steaks over the fruit and sprinkle half the pork seasoning over them. Season generously with salt and pepper.

**03** Air fry at 180ºC/360ºF for 8 minutes. Turn the pork steaks over and sprinkle with the remaining pork seasoning, along with extra salt and pepper.

**04** Air fry at the same temperature for a final 6 minutes, or until the pork steaks are firm and the fruit is fork tender.

# simple minted lamb steaks

We love pairing fresh mint and garlic with lamb and cooking it in the air fryer. Lamb steaks are another fantastic air fryer steak, and are best when spring lamb comes into season.

......................................

SERVES **4**
PREP **5 MINUTES, PLUS MARINATING TIME**
COOK TIME **10 MINUTES**
CALORIES **536**

......................................

4 × 225g/8oz lamb steaks
1 tsp dried thyme
a small bunch of fresh mint
1 tsp frozen chopped garlic
2 tsp extra virgin olive oil
2 tsp lemon juice
2 tsp clear honey
Salt and black pepper

**01** Put the lamb steaks on a plate, sprinkle them with the thyme and season generously with salt and pepper.

**02** Finely chop 2 tablespoons of fresh mint and put in a bowl with the garlic, olive oil, lemon juice and honey. Mix well, then spoon over the lamb steaks. Place the steaks into the fridge for an hour and allow to marinate.

**03** Load the steaks into the air fryer basket. Chop a little extra fresh mint and sprinkle it over the lamb steaks. Air fry at 180ºC/360ºF for 10 minutes, or until the lamb juices run clear.

# 10-minute garlic & rosemary lamb chops

**You will love lamb chops cooked in the air fryer. They are easy to prep, cook in just 10 minutes, and healthier as the excess fat drains into the bottom of the air fryer, taking it off the dinner plate.**

......................................

SERVES **2**
PREP **2 MINUTES**
COOK TIME **10 MINUTES**
CALORIES **273**

......................................

4 large lamb chops (2cm/¾in thick)
2 tsp dried thyme
2 tsp dried rosemary
6 garlic cloves
4 sprigs fresh rosemary
Salt and black pepper

**01** Place the lamb chops side by side in the air fryer basket. Season with salt and pepper and sprinkle half the dried rosemary and thyme over the chops. Peel the garlic cloves and place them in the gaps, then find some extra gaps for the fresh rosemary.

**02** Air fry the lamb chops at 180ºC/360ºF for 5 minutes, then turn the chops over with tongs. Season again with salt, pepper and the remaining dried herbs and air fry for another 5 minutes, or until the lamb juices run clear.

# easy pork-chop dinner for one

My grandad passed away a couple of weeks before we bought our first air fryer – but he would have loved it! One favourite meal my grandma always cooked him was a pork chop dinner; there would be pork chops under the grill/broiler, potatoes boiling in one pan and peas in another pan.

Instead, we are preparing everything together in the air fryer – cooking our balsamic pork chops alongside the crispy potatoes and buttered peas and sweetcorn – making it much easier for a person living alone.

......................................

SERVES **1**
PREP **8 MINUTES**
COOK TIME **22 MINUTES**
CALORIES **796**

......................................

3 medium white potatoes
2 tsp extra virgin olive oil
3 tsp dried parsley
1 bone-in pork chop (2cm/¾in thick)
2 tsp balsamic vinegar
4 tbsp frozen garden peas
4 tbsp frozen sweetcorn
2 tsp butter (chopped small chunks)
Salt and black pepper

**01** Peel the potatoes and cut them into quarters. Put them in a mixing bowl, add the olive oil and 2 teaspoons of the parsley, and season with salt and pepper. Give everything a very good mix with your hands to make sure the potatoes are well coated.

**02** Load the potatoes into the air fryer basket and spread out. Air fry at 180ºC/360ºC for 5 minutes.

**03** In the meantime, place the pork chop on a clean chopping board and smoother in balsamic vinegar, then season with the remaining parsley and salt and pepper.

**04** When the air fryer beeps, shake the potatoes, then make room next to them and add the pork chop. Air fry at the same temperature for a further 12 minutes, or until the potatoes are fork tender and the pork chop is firm to touch.

**05** Using tongs, remove the pork chop from the air fryer, place on a dinner plate and allow to rest. Shake the potatoes and create a space for the ramekin.

**06** Put the peas and sweetcorn in a ramekin with the butter and season with salt and pepper. Add the ramekin to the air fryer and cook at 160ºC/320ºF for a final 5 minutes, or until the potatoes are crispy to your liking, then serve.

**Mix and match** You can swap pork chops for other similar-sized meats – such as gammon/ham steaks, lamb chops or bacon chops – and keep the same time and temperature.

# 10-minute air fryer hot dogs

SERVES **4**
PREP **5 MINUTES**
COOK TIME **10 MINUTES**
CALORIES **270**

........................................

1 medium onion
Extra virgin olive oil spray
4 medium hot dogs
4 hot dog buns (pre-sliced)
mustard (optional)
tomato ketchup (optional)

**01** Peel and slice your onion and load into the air fryer basket. Spray the onion with olive oil, then air fry at 200°C/400°F for 3 minutes.

**02** Move the onions to the left of your air fryer basket and add your hot dogs to the right. Air fry the hot dogs and onions at 180°C/360°F for 5 minutes.

**03** Load the hot dogs into hot dog buns, top with onions and air fry for 2 minutes at 200°C/400°F. This will warm through the hot dogs, make the onions crispy and warm up your hot dog buns. If not piping hot when done, cook for an extra couple of minutes.

**04** Serve with mustard and/or ketchup for the ultimate hot dog treat.

# dom's easy cheeseburgers

SERVES **4**
PREP **5 MINUTES**
COOK TIME **12 MINUTES**
CALORIES **524**

........................................

¼ medium onion
450g/1lb minced/ground beef
2 tsp dried mixed herbs/Italian
  seasoning
2 tbsp light cream cheese
1 tsp garlic purée
4 cheese slices
Salt and black pepper

**FOR DOM'S BURGER SAUCE**
2 tbsp burger sauce/pink sauce
¼ tsp Dijon mustard
1 tsp gherkin Juice/pickle juice

**TO SERVE**
2 plum tomatoes
4 hamburger buns
Lettuce leaves
A handful of sliced pickles

**01** Peel and finely dice the onion and put it in a large mixing bowl. Add the beef, mixed herbs, cream cheese and garlic purée, and season well with salt and pepper. Mix well with your hands, breaking up the meat as you go and making sure all the seasonings are well distributed in the meat.

**02** Divide the meat into four equal portions. Use a burger press to make into hamburger patties – or just shape them in your hands.

**03** Place the burgers into the air fryer basket, spreading them out so that none overlap. Air fry at 180°C/360°F for 9 minutes, or until almost cooked through.

**04** Meanwhile, make the burger sauce by combining all the ingredients in a small bowl. Slice the plum tomatoes and set aside.

**05** When the 9 minutes is up, add a slice of cheese over each burger patty and press them down so that they don't fly off. Cook at 180°C/360°F for a further 3 minutes to melt the cheese.

**06** When the air fryer beeps, put the quarter pounders into burger buns and load them up with lettuce, sliced tomatoes and pickles, and finish with a drizzle of your burger sauce.

**07** Serve the hot dogs and burgers together with Sofia & Jorge's Corn on the Cob from page 162.

# the ultimate meat pie

We love an Aussie meat pie and it's also one of the easiest pies to prep and air fry. We make the filling with leftover beef from our pot roast (see page 168), then divide it into ramekin dishes and top each one with puff pastry to make delicious mini meat pies.

........................................

SERVES **4**
PREP **10 MINUTES**
COOK TIME **17 MINUTES**
CALORIES **343**

........................................

450g/1lb leftover roast beef or
   pulled beef
1 tbsp tomato purée/tomato
   paste
1 tbsp Worcestershire sauce,
   plus extra if needed
1 tsp garlic purée
1 sheet ready-rolled puff pastry
1 egg, beaten
Salt and black pepper

**01** Chop the leftover beef into chunks or shred the beef. Put the meat in a bowl and add the tomato purée, Worcestershire sauce and garlic purée, and season generously with salt and pepper. Mix well with a fork. If the leftovers are dry, add a little extra Worcestershire sauce.

**02** Load the meat pie filling into four small ramekins, dividing it evenly among them and filling them to almost full.

**03** Cut circles from the pastry with a cutter that's slightly larger than the top of the ramekins. Place the circles on top of the filling and press down around the edge of the ramekins to seal. Brush with the beaten egg and cut a hole in the top of each pie to allow the steam to escape during cooking.

**04** Place the ramekins into the air fryer basket and air fry at 180°C/360°F for 17 minutes, or until the centre of the pie reaches a temperature of 70°C/160°F or above.

# uncle bob's easy meatloaf

My Uncle Bob introduced me to meatloaf almost 11 years ago. My aunt joked that it was the only thing he could cook because it was so easy. I fell in love with his meatloaf, as did Dom and Kyle, and after buying our first air fryer, we converted the recipe for cooking in the air fryer. If you want an easy dinner, it doesn't get any easier than meatloaf, and the leftovers are even more amazing.

.....................................

SERVES **4**
PREP **10 MINUTES**
COOK TIME **50 MINUTES**
CALORIES **651**

.....................................

1 small onion
900g/2lb minced/ground beef
1 tsp garlic purée
1 tbsp Worcestershire sauce
2 tsp tomato purée/tomato
  paste
2 tsp dried parsley
2 tsp sweet paprika
1 tbsp dried mixed herbs/Italian
  seasoning
2 large eggs
50g/1¾oz/1 cup fresh
  breadcrumbs, plus extra
  if needed
Extra virgin olive oil spray
Salt and black pepper

## FOR THE MEATLOAF GLAZE
2 tbsp tomato ketchup
1 tsp garlic purée
2 tsp Worcestershire sauce

**01** Finely dice the onion and put it in a large mixing bowl. Add the meat, garlic purée, Worcestershire sauce, tomato purée, parsley, paprika and the dried herbs, and season well with salt and pepper. Mix well with your hands, breaking up the meat as you go and making sure all the seasonings are all well distributed in the meat.

**02** Add the eggs and breadcrumbs and mix well until you can form it into a big ball. If the mixture is too wet, add a little extra breadcrumbs.

**03** Shape your meatloaf mixture into a log and wrap it tightly in foil. Place the foil-covered meatloaf into the air fryer basket and air fry at 160ºC/320ºF for 25 minutes.

**04** Open up the foil and flatten it out around the edge of the loaf to expose the loaf, and cook at 180ºC/360ºF for a further 20 minutes or until a thermometer inserted into the centre of the meatloaf reads above 70ºC/160ºF or above.

**05** Whilst the air fryer is finishing cooking the meatloaf, mix together your glaze ingredients with a teaspoon in a little bowl.

**06** When the air fryer beeps, spray the top of the meatloaf with olive oil spray, then use the back of a spoon to spread your tomato ketchup glaze over the top of the meatloaf. Cook at 200ºC/400ºF for a further 5 minutes to warm up the glaze.

**Reheated meatloaf sandwiches** If you have leftover meatloaf, nothing is better than meatloaf sandwiches. To reheat your meatloaf, slice it and put the slices into the air fryer basket. Air fry at 160ºC/320ºF for 4 minutes. Turn the slices over with tongs and spread **1 teaspoon of tomato ketchup** on each slice. Air fry at the same temperature for a final 4 minutes, or until piping hot, before sandwiching between **slices of bread** or loading into **bread rolls**.

# minced beef (three ways)

Whether you call it minced beef or ground beef, it is so simple cooked in the air fryer and requires zero oil. You can then use it for a Bolognese sauce, taco meat, sloppy joes, and so much more.

## the basic recipe

SERVES **2**
PREP **3 MINUTES**
COOK TIME **8 MINUTES**
CALORIE **516**

..................................................

450g/1lb minced/ground beef
1 tsp frozen chopped garlic
1 tsp dried parsley
Salt and black pepper

..................................................

**01** Load your beef into the air fryer basket. Stir in the chopped garlic and parsley, and season with a sprinkle of salt and pepper.

**02** Air fry at 180ºC/360ºF for 8 minutes, or until cooked, giving it a stir with a wooden spoon at the forth minute to break up the beef; this will help it cook evenly.

**03** When the air fryer beeps, drain the liquid from the bottom, and you now have perfectly cooked minced beef ready for adding to meals.

## Make into a Fast Bolognese

Cook your beef with **½ medium diced onion**. When the mince is cooked, drain excess liquid from the air fryer and move the beef to your silicone pan. Add **1 tbsp tomato purée/tomato paste** and **500g/18oz tomato pasta sauce**, along with **1 tbsp dried basil**. Stir well, then taste and add extra salt and pepper if needed. Sprinkle with **60g/2oz/¾ cup grated Parmesan cheese** and air fry at 200ºC/400ºF for 6 minutes before serving.

## Let it be Taco Meat

Having taco Tuesday and want to keep it simple? Make our bolognese recipe (above), but substitute half the pasta sauce for **salsa** and the basil for **taco seasoning**. Leave out the Parmesan. Warm through for 8 minutes at 180ºC/360ºF, then serve in **tacos**.

## Quick Sloppy Joes

Start by peeling and finely dicing **2 large carrots**. Toss the carrots in **1 teaspoon extra virgin olive oil** and season with **salt and pepper**. Air fry at 180ºC/360ºF for 8 minutes. Move the carrots to the left of the air fryer, then follow the recipe for the bolognese above, adding the beef and onion now. When you add the pasta sauce, also add **2 tablespoons tomato ketchup, 2 tablespoons Worcestershire sauce** and forget the Parmesan. Finish by cooking at 180ºC/360ºF for 8 minutes.

**Mix and match** Swap the beef for lamb, chicken, turkey or pork and air fry in the same way.

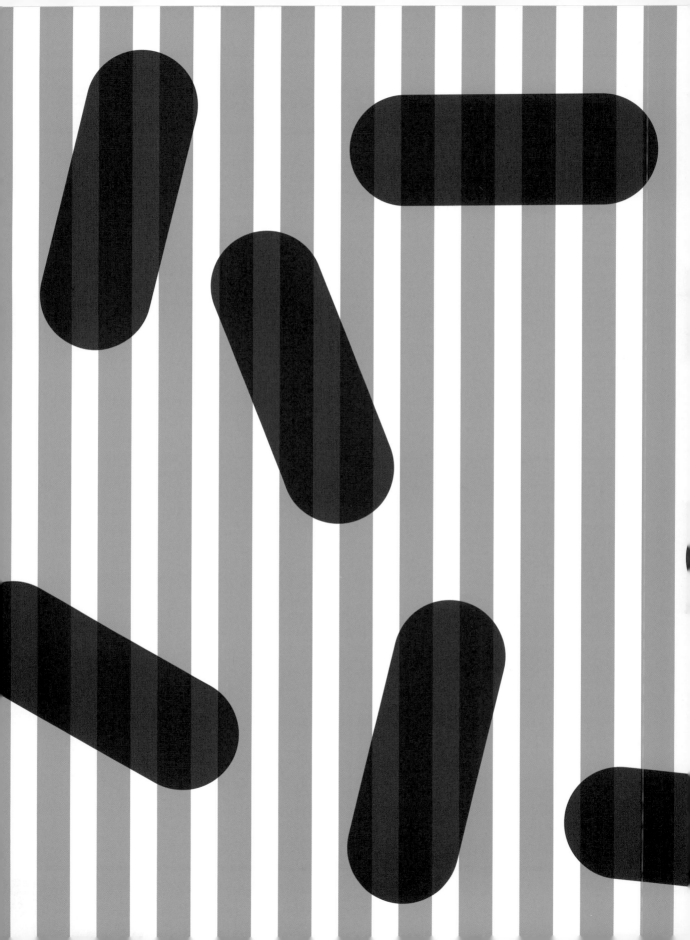

# FISH

# let's air fry fish fillets

For lunch on weekdays when the kids are at school and we are at home working, we will have fish fillets for lunch with some air fryer veggies. We love how easy it is and how quickly we can prep and cook lunch. It's also a fantastic technique to learn with your air fryer.

We recommend that you start with fish fillets and then progress to cooking veggies at the same time. For learning this technique, we are going to show you how to air fry salmon, but you can mix and match with fillets of other fish, too.

# quick & easy air fried salmon fillets

We wait until salmon is on a special deal, then bulk buy and freeze for later. We either defrost the night before or cook straight from frozen.

SERVES **2**
PREP **2 MINUTES**
COOK TIME **8 MINUTES**
CALORIES **256**

2 × 115g/4oz salmon fillets
Extra virgin olive oil spray
1 slice of lemon
1 tsp dried dill
Salt and black pepper

**01** Place the salmon fillets into the air fryer basket. Spray them with olive oil and squeeze a slice of lemon over the two fillets. Sprinkle with dill and season with salt and pepper.

**02** Air fry the salmon at 180ºC/360ºF for 8 minutes, or until the fish is firm to the touch.

### Reheating Salmon

You can reheat cooked salmon fillets in the air fryer at 160ºC/320ºF for 6 minutes.

### Swap the Salmon

You can use the same recipe and swap salmon for any other similar-sized boneless fish fillets, such as sea bass, haddock, cod, tilapia, catfish or pollock.

### Cooking Fish from Frozen

You can also cook fish fillets from frozen in the air fryer. We found the ideal time and temperature is 180ºC/360ºF for 15 minutes.

### Fish and Veggies

With the cooking time for fish fillets being 8 minutes, you can use the vegetable cooking times list  on page 150, find a vegetable with a similar cooking time and cook both the fish and vegetables together. Or if you have a vegetable that is 4 minutes longer, cook the vegetable for 4 minutes before adding the salmon. A good example of this is our salmon bowl on page 98.

### Salmon of Many Flavours

**Teriyaki** You can add a drizzle of teriyaki sauce to the top of your salmon instead of the olive oil and it will be as if you are at a Chinese restaurant.

**Honey, garlic & mustard** Make our chicken thigh glaze (page 56) and brush the glaze over the salmon for the last 4 minutes of the cook time.

**Lemon & garlic**  Swap the olive oil for lemon juice, and add 1 teaspoon of lemon zest and 1 teaspoon of garlic purée.

# quick prep whole tilapia

**Tilapia is our favourite whole fish to air fry. It perfectly fits most air fryers, and you will love how easy it is to prep and how tender the flakes of fish are.**

....................................................

SERVES **2**
PREP **5 MINUTES**
COOK TIME **22 MINUTES**
CALORIES **163**

....................................................

1 whole black tilapia, gutted
   and scaled
1 lemon, sliced
2 garlic cloves (sliced)
2 tsp chopped fresh curly
   parsley
2 tsp chopped fresh dill
2 tsp fresh thyme
1 tbsp extra virgin olive oil
1 tsp dried parsley
Salt and black pepper

**01** Check that your whole fish has clear eyes (a sign of freshness), then cut off the fins with a pair of scissors. Slice the lemon and garlic cloves and stuff the slices inside the fish, along with the fresh herbs.

**02** Score the sides of the fish with a sharp knife, making three slashes on each side of the fish which cut through the skin and slightly into the flesh. Drizzle over the extra virgin olive oil and rub in all over, then sprinkle with the parsley and season with salt and pepper.

**03** Place the whole fish in the air fryer, set the temperature to 180ºC/360ºF and cook for 22 minutes, or until the fish is cooked through and flakes on touch.

# grandad george's homemade herby fishcakes

My Grandad George was a fisherman and an amazing cook too. I loved the frugal meals he made and my all-time favourite was his delicious fishcakes.

Preparing fishcakes in the air fryer is simple thanks to cooking the potatoes and fish first, making into fish patties and then air frying to crisp up.

........................................

MAKES **10**
PREP **12 MINUTES**
COOK TIME **39 MINUTES**
CALORIES **225**

........................................

900g/2lb medium white
   potatoes
2 tsp dried thyme
1 tbsp extra virgin olive oil
450g/1lb boneless and skinless
   fish fillets, such as pollock,
   cod or haddock
½ red onion
1 tbsp mixed herbs/Italian
   seasoning
1 tbsp dried parsley
28g/1oz melted butter
4 tbsp whole/full-fat milk
4 tbsp oat flour, plus
   90g/3¼oz/⅔ cup, for coating
Juice of 1 lemon
1 tbsp dried barbecue
   seasoning (optional)
Salt and black pepper

**01** Peel the potatoes, dice them into chunks and put in a mixing bowl. Season with salt and pepper and add the thyme and olive oil. Mix well with your hands.

**02** Tip the potatoes into the air fryer basket and spread out. Air fry at 180ºC/360ºF for 15 minutes, or until fork tender. Transfer them to a food processor.

**03** Place the fish fillets into the air fryer basket, season with salt and pepper and air fry at 180ºC/360ºF for 8 minutes, or until the fish flakes on touch.

**04** While the fish is cooking, finely dice the onion and put it in the food processor with the potatoes. Add the mixed herbs, parsley, melted butter, milk, 4 tablespoons oat flour and the lemon juice. Once cooked, add the fish and pulse a few times until the ingredients are broken down and combined but still a little chunky.

**05** Put the oat flour for coating in a shallow bowl, add the barbecue seasoning, if using (this will give them a golden glow in the air fryer), and mix with a fork.

**06** Divide the potato and fish mixture into 10 equal portions and shape them into patties. Roll each fish cake in the oat flour to create a thin coating which will stop them sticking in the air fryer.

**07** Place up to four fishcakes into the air fryer basket. Air fry at 180ºC/360ºF for 8 minutes, then turn over with tongs and air fry for another 8 minutes, or until piping hot and crispy. Repeat to cook the remaining fish cakes.

**Freezer friendly fishcakes** My mum taught me to make at least 10, then freeze the remaining. Once thawed, you can reheat them in the air fryer at 180ºC/360ºF for 4 minutes on each side, or until piping hot throughout (or if you have frozen them uncooked, just let them thaw, then follow the cooking directions above).

**Mix it up!** You can swap the white fish for salmon, crab or even tuna for a different flavoured fishcake. As a kid, my mum and I would buy a selection of fish scraps from the local fisherman to make them.

# friday night fish & chips

We grew up in a seaside town famous for its fish and chips. It was a staple meal growing up, and still is now. No surprise that when we got our first air fryer it was one of the first recipes we converted to the air fryer. If you love fish and chips, you will love this easy air fryer version.

......................................

SERVES **2**
PREP **8 MINUTES**
COOK TIME **23 MINUTES**
CALORIES **842**

......................................

**FOR THE CHIPS**
3 medium potatoes
1 tbsp extra virgin olive oil
2 tsp dried parsley
2 tsp dried dill

**FOR THE FISH**
2 cod fillets
2 eggs, beaten
2 tbsp lemon juice
130g/4½oz/1 cup plain
 (all-purpose) flour
5 tsp dried parsley
100g/3½oz/2 cups fresh
 breadcrumbs
2 tsp dried dill
2 tsp dried basil
Salt and black pepper

**01** Sit the cod fillets on kitchen paper/paper towels and allow the excess moisture to soak into the towels.

**02** Peel the potatoes and slice them into chips. Put them in a bowl with the rest of the chip ingredients, season with salt and pepper and mix well with your hands.

**03** Tip the chips into the air fryer basket and spread them out. Air fry at 160ºC/320ºF for 8 minutes.

**04** Whilst you are waiting, set up your production line. Combine the beaten egg and lemon juice in one shallow bowl. In the second bowl, combine the flour and 1 tablespoon of parsley. In the final bowl, combine the breadcrumbs, the remaining parsley, the dried dill and basil and a generous amount of salt and pepper. For easy breading, make sure the contents of all bowls are well mixed and that they are laid out in order of flour, egg, then breadcrumbs.

**05** Place the cod fillets onto a chopping board, and season well with salt and pepper.

**06** Turn the fish fillets over in the flour so that they are coated all over. Next, dip them into the egg to fully coat and finally, using your other hand to keep things from getting too messy, turn them in the breadcrumbs until well coated.

**07** When the air fryer beeps, place the fish over the chips and air fry at 180ºC/360ºF for a further 8 minutes.

**08** Once the 8 minutes is up, remove the chips from the basket and cook the fish on its own at 200ºC/400ºF for 7 minutes to crisp it up before serving.

# rainbow salmon bowls

**This is another of our favourite healthy air fryer bowls; salmon, sweet potato and vegetables are cooked in one air fryer basket. Served together in one bowl, they make a delicious healthy lunch for two.**

SERVES **2**
PREP **10 MINUTES**
COOK TIME **22 MINUTES**
CALORIES **538**

1 medium sweet potato
1 medium courgette/zucchini
1 red (bell) pepper/capsicum
3 spring onions/scallions
2 tsp tomato purée/paste
1 tsp balsamic vinegar
1 tsp dried basil
1 tbsp lemon juice
280g/10oz boneless and
  skinless salmon fillets
  (2½ fillets)
1 tsp dried dill
115g/4oz/1 cup drained canned
  chickpeas (about ½ can)
1 tsp extra virgin olive oil
1 tsp smoked paprika
1 tsp garlic purée
A pinch of ground cumin
Salt and black pepper
Fresh basil leaves, to serve
  (optional)

**01** Peel and dice the sweet potato. Dice the courgette and deseed and dice the red pepper. Dice the spring onions into 1cm/½ inch slices.

**02** Place the vegetables in a bowl and add 1 teaspoon of the tomato purée, the balsamic vinegar, basil, and ½ tablespoon of the lemon juice. Season well with salt and pepper and mix well with your hands.

**03** Tip the veg into the air fryer and spread out. Air fry at 180ºC/360ºF for 12 minutes.

**04** In the meantime, on a chopping board, chop each salmon fillet into four evenly sized cubes, then chop the remaining half a fillet into two. Drizzle them with the remaining lemon juice, sprinkle with dill and season with salt and pepper.

**05** When the air fryer beeps, shake the air fryer, move the vegetables to the left of the air fryer basket and add the salmon bites to the right. Air fry at the same temperature for 4 minutes.

**06** While the salmon cooks, put the chickpeas in a bowl with the remaining 1 teaspoon tomato purée, the olive oil, smoked paprika, garlic purée and cumin. Season with salt and pepper and mix with a fork.

**07** When the air fryer beeps, add the chickpeas to the basket, sprinkling them over the vegetables, and cook for 6 more minutes, or until the vegetables are crispy, the salmon is cooked through and the chickpeas are almost crispy.

**08** Divide everything between two bowls, sprinkle with basil leaves, if using, and enjoy warm.

# super-easy tuna niçoise

One of my favourite salads when eating out in France is tuna niçoise. It's a delicious tuna salad but a real effort to recreate at home. But thanks to the air fryer, you can make it super easy and do all the cooking in one air fryer basket.

....................................

SERVES **2**
PREP **15 MINUTES**
COOK TIME **23 MINUTES**
CALORIES **467**

....................................

2 large eggs
85g/3oz green beans
Extra virgin olive oil spray
2 tsp dried dill
8 red baby potatoes
1 tsp extra virgin olive oil
1 tsp dried parsley
150g/5½oz/2 cups shredded
   lettuce
10 pitted black olives
10 cherry tomatoes
2 × 115g/4oz boneless and
   skinless tuna steaks
a squeeze of lemon juice

## FOR THE SALAD DRESSING
1 tsp lemon juice
1 tsp extra virgin olive oil
1 tsp garlic purée
1 tsp dried dill
Salt and black pepper

**01** Place the eggs to the left of the air fryer basket. Trim the green beans, if necessary, then add them to the right side of the basket. Spray the green beans with olive oil and sprinkle with half the dill.

**02** Scrub the baby potatoes, then put them in a bowl with the 1 teaspoon of olive oil and the dried parsley. Season with salt and pepper and mix with your hands. Find a spare gap in the air fryer basket and add the potatoes, making sure that they don't cover the eggs or the beans. Air fry the eggs, green beans and potatoes together at 120ºC/250ºF for 14 minutes.

**03** In the meantime, make the salad dressing. Mix all the dressing ingredients in a small bowl with a spoon. Season with salt and pepper and put to one side.

**04** Scatter the lettuce over an oval salad bowl or serving platter and top with the olives. Halve the cherry tomatoes and scatter these over, too.

**05** When the air fryer beeps, remove the eggs and put them in a bowl of cold water until cool enough to handle.

**06** Add the tuna steaks to the air fryer in the space where the eggs were. Season the tuna with salt and pepper, add a squeeze of lemon juice, and sprinkle over the remaining dill. Air fry at 180ºC/360ºF for 5 minutes.

**07** Meanwhile, peel the eggs, slice them in half and add to the salad platter. When the air fryer beeps, remove the green beans and add those to the salad too.

**08** Air fry the tuna steaks and the potatoes at 180ºC/360ºF for a final 4 minutes, or until the potatoes are golden and crispy and the tuna is firm to the touch.

**09** Slice the tuna steaks into strips and add the tuna and potatoes to the salad. Drizzle with the salad dressing before serving.

# taco tuesday prawn tacos

**Whether you call them king prawns or shrimp, you can air fry peeled prawns from frozen, make a delicious avocado crema and serve them for your next taco Tuesday.**

......................................

MAKES **4**
PREP **10 MINUTES**
COOK TIME **9 MINUTES**
CALORIES **297**

......................................

1 lime
225g/8oz peeled raw frozen
   king prawns/shrimp
½ small red onion
¼ medium red cabbage
1 spring onion/scallion
1 large avocado
1 tbsp salsa
1 tsp ground cumin
2 tsp taco seasoning
1 tsp sweet paprika
A pinch of cayenne pepper
1 recipe quantity Avocado
   Crema (see page 120)
8 small corn tacos, or 4 tortilla
   wraps
Salt and black pepper

**01** Cut your lime into wedges. Load the frozen prawns into the air fryer basket along with the lime wedges and air fry at 180ºC/360ºF for 6 minutes.

**02** In the meantime, peel and dice the red onion. Wash and shred the red cabbage. Clean and slice the spring onion. Peel and slice the avocado.

**03** When the air fryer beeps, remove the almost-cooked prawns and put them into a bowl with the salsa, cumin, taco seasoning, sweet paprika and cayenne. Season with salt and pepper and mix with a spoon.

**04** Tip the prawns back into the air fryer and air fry for a further 3 minutes or until the prawns are cooked.

**05** Spread avocado crema over the tacos and add a spoonful of the prawns. Top with sliced avocado and a drizzle more crema, then cover with red cabbage and onion and serve.

# VEGETARIAN
# & VEGAN

# let's air fry tofu

An excellent starting point to meat-free cooking in the air fryer is tofu. It's so easy to prepare and then air fry, and you can mix and match seasonings. We like it best on a cobb salad (page 110).

225g/8oz firm tofu
1 tsp white wine vinegar
1 tsp extra virgin olive oil
½ tsp garlic powder
1 tsp dried parsley
1 tsp dried basil
Salt and black pepper

SERVES **2**
PREP **8 MINUTES, PLUS PRESSING**
COOK TIME **10 MINUTES**
CALORIES **196**

**01** Line a large plate with a tea towel/dish towel. Remove the tofu from its packaging, place it on the plate and add another tea towel on top. Place a heavy object over it and put it to one side for 2 hours while the liquid is pressed out of the tofu.

**02** In the meantime, put all the other ingredients in a bowl, season with salt and pepper and mix well.

**03** When the 2 hours are up, discard the tea towels, place your tofu on a chopping board and cut into cubes. Put the cubes into the marinade bowl and mix with your hands until every piece of tofu is well coated.

**04** Place the tofu in the air fryer basket and spread out. Air fry at 180ºC/360ºF for 6 minutes.

**05** Shake the tofu, then cook at 200ºC/400ºF for a further 4 minutes, or until crispy to your liking, then serve.

# seriously satisfying vegan cobb salad

We first tried a cobb salad at the Hollywood Brown Derby more than a decade ago and fell in love with the concept of neat rows of salad ingredients over lettuce. This is our vegan version.

........................................

SERVES **2**
PREP **10 MINUTES**
COOK TIME **10 MINUTES**
CALORIES **737**

........................................

**FOR THE DRESSING**
1 tsp garlic purée
1 tbsp white wine vinegar
1 tbsp balsamic vinegar
1 tbsp maple syrup
½ tbsp extra virgin olive oil

**FOR THE SALAD**
225g/8oz firm tofu, pressed (see page 108)
115g/4oz drained canned chickpeas (about ½ x 400g/14oz can)
165g/5¾oz/1 cup frozen sweetcorn
½ iceberg lettuce
½ red onion
10 cherry tomatoes
2 medium avocados
Salt and black pepper

**01** Put all the dressing ingredients in a small bowl and mix with a tablespoon.

**02** Cut the pressed tofu into cubes and put them in a bowl. Add 1 tablespoon of the dressing and toss to coat. Place the tofu cubes in the air fryer basket and air fry at 180°C/360°F for 5 minutes.

**03** While the tofu cooks, combine the chickpeas and ½ tablespoon of the dressing in a small bowl and stir with a spoon.

**04** In another small bowl, combine the sweetcorn with a tablespoon of the dressing and stir.

**05** Next, prepare the rest of your salad. Wash and shred the lettuce, peel and dice the onion and cut the cherry tomatoes in half. Halve the avocados and remove the stone/pits, then peel and slice them.

**06** When the air fryer beeps, move the tofu to the far left of the air fryer basket and tip the chickpeas and corn into the space in the right-hand side. Cook at the same temperature for a further 5 minutes, or until the tofu and chickpeas are crispy.

**07** While everything cooks, assemble the salad. Spoon the remaining salad dressing into a serving bowl, then add the shredded lettuce in a layer on top to cover the whole dish. Toss the lettuce so that the dressing coats the lettuce. Now start adding the rows of salad ingredients that make a cobb salad distinctive: add a line of red onion, followed by a line of tomatoes, then a line of avocado.

**08** Once cooked, add separate rows of the tofu, chickpeas and sweetcorn to your salad. Season with salt and pepper and serve.

# perfect halloumi fajitas

**Air fried halloumi cheese makes a fantastic vegetarian alternative to chicken. Once cooked, the halloumi will have a firm texture similar to grilled chicken. Because of this, it is perfect for fajitas.**

................................................

SERVES **2**
PREP **8 MINUTES**
COOK TIME **14 MINUTES**
CALORIES **461**

................................................

1 red (bell) pepper/capsicum
1 orange (bell) pepper/
   capsicum
1 green (bell) pepper/capsicum
1 small red onion
1 tsp extra virgin olive oil
1 tbsp fajita seasoning
225g/8oz halloumi cheese
Salt and black pepper

**TO SERVE (OPTIONAL)**
Tortilla wraps
Sour cream
Fresh coriander/cilantro

**01** Halve and deseed the peppers and slice them lengthways. Peel and slice the onion, lengthways. Put them both in a bowl and add the olive oil and fajita seasoning. Season with salt and pepper and mix well.

**02** Pat the halloumi dry with kitchen towel and slice it lengthways into strips. Gently add the halloumi to the bowl and mix in, being careful not to break the strips.

**03** Load the fajita ingredients into the air fryer basket and spread them out. Air fry at 180°C/360°F for 12 minutes. Shake the fajitas, then cook at 200°C/400°F for a final 2 minutes.

**04** Serve in a big bowl as a fajita salad, or load into wraps with a spoonful of sour cream. Sprinkle with fresh coriander, if you like.

# sticky vegetable stir-fry with noodles

Forget standing over a wok and waiting for the stir-fry to cook.

With the air fryer method, you load veggies into the air fryer and make a quick stir-fry sauce as the veggies cook, then it all comes together in the air fryer.

.........................................

SERVES **2**
PREP **12 MINUTES**
COOK TIME **21 MINUTES**
CALORIES **366**

.........................................

1 red (bell) pepper/capsicum
1 orange (bell) pepper/capsicum
3 medium carrots
1 small red onion
150g/5½oz trimmed green beans
2 tsp extra virgin olive oil
2 tsp Chinese 5-spice powder
115g/4oz fresh egg noodles
Salt and black pepper

**FOR THE STIR-FRY SAUCE**
1½ tbsp clear honey or maple syrup
2 tbsp soy sauce
1 tsp rice vinegar
2 tsp garlic purée
1 tsp ginger purée
1 tsp lemongrass purée

**01** Halve and deseed the red and orange peppers and slice into long strips. Peel the carrots and onion and slice them into strips. Put all these in a bowl with the trimmed green beans and add olive oil and Chinese 5-spice powder. Season with salt and pepper and mix with your hands until all the veggies are well coated.

**02** Load the mixed stir-fry veggies into the air fryer and spread out. Air fry at 180°C/360°F for 16 minutes, or until the veggies have shrunk in size and the carrots are fork tender.

**03** Whilst the veggies are air frying, put all the stir-fry sauce ingredients in a bowl and mix with a spoon. Put it to one side.

**04** When the air fryer beeps, load the veggies into a silicone pan with handles. Add the stir-fry sauce and noodles and mix with tongs so everything is evenly coated with the sauce.

**05** Place the veggie stir-fry (still in its silicone pan) back into the air fryer basket and air fry at 180°C/360°F for a final 5 minutes, or until the noodles are warmed through.

# the best vegetarian lasagne

We love a vegetarian lasagne, but we can never decide if we prefer one loaded with roasted veggies or cheesy spinach. Instead, we have made a layer of each for the best vegetarian lasagne.

........................................

SERVES **4**
PREP **15 MINUTES, PLUS MAKING THE CHEESE SAUCE**
COOK TIME **45 MINUTES**
CALORIES **434**

........................................

¼ medium butternut squash
½ medium courgette/zucchini
½ red (bell) pepper/capsicum
2 spring onions/scallions
1 tbsp extra virgin olive oil
½ tsp garlic powder
2 tsp dried oregano
1 × 400g/14oz can chopped
   tomatoes
2 tsp garlic purée
2 tsp tomato purée/tomato
   paste
6 fresh basil leaves
2 tsp dried thyme
2 tsp dried mixed herbs/Italian
   seasoning
12 fresh lasagne sheets
100g/3½oz frozen spinach,
   thawed and drained
225g/8oz/2 cups grated
   mozzarella cheese
250g/9oz/1 cup ricotta cheese
2 tsp dried basil
4 tbsp Quick Hidden-Veggie
   Cheese Sauce (see page 175)
Salt and black pepper

**01** Peel and dice the butternut squash. Dice the courgette and pepper, and slice the spring onions. Put them all in a bowl with the olive oil, garlic powder and oregano and season generously with salt and pepper. Mix well with your hands so that all the veggies are evenly coated, then load them into the air fryer basket. Air fry at 180ºC/360ºF for 20 minutes, or until the squash is fork tender.

**02** In the meantime, put the tomatoes, garlic purée, tomato purée, basil, thyme and mixed herbs into a blender and pulse until smooth.

**03** Spoon 3 tablespoons of the tomato sauce into the bottom of a deep silicone pan with handles and spread out with the back of the spoon. Arrange a layer of lasagne sheets on top to cover the whole dish, tearing them up into smaller pieces to fill any gaps.

**04** Put the remaining tomato sauce into a bowl. When the air fryer beeps, add the cooked veggies to the bowl and mix. Spoon the veggie layer over the lasagne sheets and spread out evenly, then add another layer of lasagne sheets on top.

**05** Put the defrosted spinach in a bowl, making sure a final squeeze is done first to remove any extra moisture. Add all but 50g/1¾oz/¼ cup of the mozzarella, and all the ricotta and dried basil and season with salt and pepper. Mix well with a fork.

**06** Spoon the spinach mixture over the lasagne sheets in the dish and spread evenly, then add another layer of lasagne sheets. Spoon over the cheese sauce, then finish by sprinkling the remaining grated mozzarella over the top.

**07** Place the silicone pan into the air fryer by its handles. Air fry the lasagne at 180ºC/360ºF for 15 minutes. Turn the temperature down to 160ºC/320ºF and give it another 10 minutes, or until the top is golden and the lasagne is piping hot throughout.

**Using dried lasagne?** Dried lasagne takes much longer to cook and can be rather starchy. If it's all you have, soak the dried lasagne sheets in cold water for 90 minutes before using. Soaking will give the dried sheets the same texture as fresh raw pasta and will remove a lot of the starch, making the lasagne taste much better.

# superhero hidden-veggie burgers

These vegan burgers came about when we had leftover veggies and lentils, so we mashed them together and they made amazing veggie burgers. Now we roast extra veggies in the air fryer just to make them.

.......................................

MAKES **6**
PREP **10 MINUTES**
COOK TIME **27 MINUTES**
CALORIES **488**

.......................................

3 large carrots
1 large sweet potato
1 red (bell) pepper/capsicum
2 tbsp extra virgin olive oil
1 tsp dried basil
1 tbsp dried oregano
65g/2¼oz/½ cup cooked
   green lentils
2 tbsp vegan mayonnaise
3 spring onions/scallions
   (sliced)
1 tsp garlic purée
1 tbsp dried mixed herbs/Italian
   seasoning
180g/6¼oz/2 cups oat flour
Salt and black pepper

**TO SERVE**
Burger buns
Salad of your choice
Dom's Burger Sauce (see
   page 80)

**01** Peel and dice the carrots and sweet potato and put in a bowl. Halve and deseed the red pepper, dice it and add to the bowl. Add the olive oil, basil and oregano and mix well with your hands so that the vegetables are evenly coated. Tip into the air fryer and air fry at 180ºC/360ºF for 15 minutes, or until fork tender.

**02** Add the cooked vegetables to a food processor along with the lentils, mayonnaise, spring onions, garlic purée and mixed herbs. Season with salt and pepper and pulse until you have a mushy consistency.

**03** Tip the mixture onto a floured worktop, flour your hands and add enough of the remaining flour to bind everything together and stop it sticking.

**04** Divide the mixture into six equal portions, then shape them into patties in a burger press, or just in the palms of your hands.

**05** Load four burgers into the air fryer basket. Air fry at 200ºC/400ºF for 12 minutes, or until crispy and heated through. Then repeat to air fry the final two.

**06** Place your burgers into burger buns and add your preferred burger garnish and burger sauce.

# date-night vegan burrito bowls

Burrito bowls are one of our favourite healthier dinners on a busy weeknight. We can just grab ingredients from the fridge, load items that need cooking into the air fryer and prep as the air fryer cooks. They are even more special with our fun burrito bowls.

........................................

SERVES **2**
PREP **12 MINUTES**
COOK TIME **17 MINUTES**
CALORIES **842**

........................................

2 wheat tortilla wraps (optional)
225g/8oz firm tofu, pressed
  (see page 108)
2 tsp taco seasoning (see page
  120 for homemade)
1 tsp extra virgin olive oil
1 red (bell) pepper/capsicum
8 tbsp frozen sweetcorn
8 tbsp drained, canned black
  beans
12 cherry tomatoes, halved
6 tbsp salsa
Salt and black pepper

## FOR THE VEGAN AVOCADO CREMA

1 avocado
Finely grated zest and juice
  of 1 lime
120ml/4fl oz/½ cup coconut
  milk
1 tsp dried coriander/cilantro
  leaf
1 tsp garlic purée

**01**  If you are making edible bowls, prepare these first. Use a tortilla wrap to line a cereal bowl, folding about four tucks into the tortilla as you go so that it fits the bowl perfectly. Place a ramekin inside the moulded tortilla to keep it in shape. Repeat to line a second bowl with a tortilla, weighing the wrap down with another ramekin. Place the wraps, in their bowl moulds, into the air fryer basket and air fry at 180ºC/360ºF for 5 minutes. Remove the ramekin carefully (it will be hot) and air fry for a further 2 minutes, or until the tortillas are crisp and golden and holding their bowl shape.

**02**  Chop the pressed tofu into cubes and put them in a bowl with the taco seasoning. Season with salt and pepper and add the olive oil. Mix with your hands until the tofu is evenly coated, then load into the air fryer basket to the left, leaving some space on the right of the basket.

**03**  Next, deseed the pepper and chop into cubes. Add them to the right of the air fryer basket. Air fry at 180ºC/360ºF for 5 minutes.

**04**  Shake the tofu and peppers, then find a space and add the frozen corn. Air fry at the same temperature for a final 5 minutes, or until the corn is starting to crisp.

**05**  While the tofu, corn and pepper cook, make the avocado crema. Add all the ingredients to a blender and pulse until smooth.

**06**  To assemble your burrito bowls, arrange all the filling ingredients – the black beans, corn, tofu, peppers, cherry tomatoes and salsa into your tortilla bowls – keeping them in separate little piles. If you haven't made the bowls, just arrange the elements in a large cereal bowl, or similar. Drizzle the avocado crema over the burrito bowl and serve.

# cheese toasties

Whether you live in the UK and call them cheese toasties or live in the US and call it grilled cheese, it is so delicious cooked in the air fryer. You can also adapt this master recipe and add in other favourites, such as sliced tomatoes or red onion. We like to serve our cheese toasties with mayonnaise for dunking or with a bowl of tomato soup.

Butter or mayonnaise, softened, for spreading
4 slices white bread
2 large slices Cheddar cheese

SERVES **2**   PREP **5 MINUTES**   COOK TIME **7 MINUTES**   CALORIES **566**

**01** Preheat the air fryer to 200ºC/400ºF for 3 minutes.

**02** Spread the butter or mayonnaise over the tops of the slices of bread.

**03** Place two slices of bread in the air fryer, butter side down. Add a slice of cheese on top of each, then sandwich with the remaining two slices of bread, butter side up. Press down to make sure the sandwiches stay in position.

**04** Air fry for 5 minutes at 200ºC/400ºF, then flip the sandwiches over and cook at the same temperature for a further 2 minutes, or until crispy to your liking.

**05** Slice each toastie into halves or quarters and serve.

# crispy curried chickpeas

This is Jorge's favourite air fryer snack. If he wants comfort food, he will air fry these. A reader favourite, many readers compare them to roasted peanuts, but they are a nut-free, healthier option.

1 × 400g/14oz can chickpeas
1 tbsp extra virgin olive oil
1 tsp ground cumin
1 tsp smoked paprika
½ tsp garam masala
Salt and black pepper

SERVES **2**   PREP **3 MINUTES**   COOK TIME **7 MINUTES**   CALORIES **208**

**01** Drain the chickpeas into a sieve, then rinse them under a cold tap. Pat dry with a kitchen towel/paper towel.

**02** Put the chickpeas into a mixing bowl and add the oil, cumin, paprika and garam masala. Season with salt and pepper and mix well with your hands.

**03** Tip the chickpeas into the air fryer basket and spread out in a single layer. Air fry at 180ºC/360ºF for 7 minutes, or until crispy to your liking.

# three-ingredient cajun tortilla chips

One of our favourite air fryer snacks is tortilla chips. Using mini tortilla wraps, a little oil and your favourite seasoning, they are fast, they are crispy and they are addictive.

......................................

SERVES **2**
PREP **5 MINUTES**
COOK TIME **10 MINUTES**
CALORIES **503**

......................................

5 tbsp extra virgin olive oil
4 tsp Cajun seasoning
4 mini tortilla wraps
Salsa, to serve

**01** Combine the olive oil and Cajun seasoning in a ramekin or small bowl and mix well with a fork.

**02** Place a tortilla wrap on a clean chopping board. Use a pastry brush to brush a layer of Cajun oil on one side of the tortilla wrap. Turn it over and do the same on the other side. Repeat to coat the other wraps.

**03** Using scissors, cut a wrap in half, then in half again and in half again. Then do the same again with the other half of the wrap. This will then create eight triangles per wrap. Repeat for the other two wraps.

**04** Load the triangles into the air fryer and air fry at 180ºC/360ºF for 5 minutes.

**05** Remove the crispy tortilla chips from the top and put to one side. Turn over those left at the bottom and air fry at the same temperature for a final 5 minutes, or until crispy enough.

**06** Serve with salsa.

**For loaded nachos** Mix **a jar of salsa** with the **taco meat** on page 84 and serve over the tortilla chips with **grated cheese** for quick air fryer loaded nachos.

# POTATOES

# which potato varieties are worthy of air frying?

Quite often we will buy a cheap bag of white potatoes when shopping. That same bag will do roast potatoes for a Sunday roast, chips for the kids and any leftovers will become cubed potatoes. You can of course do this, especially to keep the cost down, but you might want the best potatoes for the air fryer, rather than the cheapest.

If that is the case, the number one potato for air frying is the red potato. This is because red potatoes have less starch and never get dry as you air fry, and they are very waxy, meaning they keep their shape. We were first introduced to red potatoes in Portugal by a nutritionist, who told us how red potatoes are also healthier than standard white potatoes as they contain the higher levels of vitamins and minerals.

After red potatoes, another good waxy potato choice is fingerling.

The in-between choice (which is partly starchy) is Yukon Gold, which creates the best air fryer roast potato.

If you do opt for starchy potatoes like Maris Piper, King Edward or russet, it is advised that you soak in water before air frying to remove some of the starch, which you don't need to do with the waxy varieties.

Sweet potatoes do fall into the floury potatoes category, but are delicious in the air fryer so we recommend bulk buying when in season.

Having said all this, if Dom had his way, he would maintain that the potatoes with eyes are best in the air fryer because of the softness – so don't be worried if you have a few that have been lingering in the veg rack too long!

Now we have given you a potato run through, let's air fry some potatoes.

## Top Tips

**Got a slower air fryer?** Add an extra 5 minutes to the cook time at 180ºC/360ºF.

**Not all chip size is equal.** You have thick cut steak chips, skinny French fries, shoestring fries and many others. Our cook time is for medium-thickness chips. Reduce the cook time for skinny and increase it for thick steak cut.

**Cooking frozen chips?** See the frozen chips guide on page 20.

**Making fries for one?** Quarter the ingredients and cook for 15 minutes at 160ºC/320ºF, shake and spray, then cook for a final 5 minutes at 200ºC/400ºF

**Don't overfill the air fryer** Your chips will take much longer to cook, stick together and will lack a crispy texture. It is much better to make two batches.

**Turn up the heat** The art of perfect air fryer chips is all about three temperatures: 160ºC/320ºF to kick start the chips, 180ºC/360ºF to cook the chips and 200ºC/400ºF to crisp them up.

## Let's Try to Make Dry Potatoes Amazing

If you only have potatoes that are out of season and really dry, or floury potatoes, we recommend that you follow our homemade chips recipe but make a few modifications:

- Soak the chips in a bowl of cold water first, then drain and pat dry.
- Double up the extra virgin olive oil and use 2 tablespoons instead of 1 tablespoon.
- Shake the air fryer basket every 5 minutes to help free chips that are stuck together.
- Avoid a 200ºC/400ºF temperature; instead, do 12 minutes at 160ºC/320ºF, followed by 15 minutes at 180ºC/360ºF.

# simple air fryer homemade chips

Whether you call them chips, French fries or *frites*, they are the reason most people buy an air fryer. We put ourselves in the most people list; we were intrigued by the idea of chips that are crispy (like you'd enjoy when eating out) but with the calorie count of a jacket potato.

First we are going to show you a simple technique, followed by some delicious variations on it – for sweet potato or even your favourite veggies.

SERVES **4**
PREP **10 MINUTES**
COOK TIME **25 MINUTES**
CALORIES **391**

8 medium white potatoes
1 tbsp extra virgin olive oil
1½ tsp dried oregano
Salt and black pepper
Extra virgin olive oil spray

Peel the potatoes and slice them into chips/fries. Aim for a universal size so that they cook evenly.

Put the chips into a mixing bowl and add the olive oil and oregano, and season with salt and pepper. Mix the ingredients well with your hands so that the chips are evenly coated.

Load the chips into the air fryer basket. Air fry at 160ºC/320ºC for 15 minutes, giving them a shake after 8 minutes to stop them sticking together. When the air fryer beeps, shake again and then spray with olive oil.

Increase the temperature to 180ºC/360ºF and cook for another 5 minutes, until fork tender. Shake the chips, spray again and cook at 200ºC/400ºF for a final 5 minutes, or until the chips are crispy to your liking.

Are you team white potato or team sweet potato? Whilst Dom and Sofia prefer white, Jorge and I love to share a bowl of sweet potato chips/fries with some aioli (see page 133).

1 large sweet potato
1 tbsp extra virgin olive oil
1½ tsp sweet paprika
Salt and black pepper

# sweet potato chips

SERVES **2**   PREP **10 MINUTES**   COOK TIME **20 MINUTES**   CALORIES **270**

**01** Peel the sweet potato and slice it into chips/fries. Aim for a universal size so that they cook evenly.

**02** Put the sweet potato chips into a mixing bowl and add the olive oil and sweet paprika, and season with salt and pepper. Mix the ingredients well with your hands so that the chips are evenly coated.

**03** Load the sweet potato chips into the air fryer basket and spread out. Air fry at 160°C/320°F for 15 minutes. Give them a shake, then increase the temperature to 200°C/400°F and cook for another 5 minutes, or until crispy at the edges.

**Keep it cubed!** If you'd rather do diced sweet potato instead of chips, peel and dice **1 large sweet potato**. Put it in a mixing bowl with **1 tablespoon extra virgin olive oil** and **2 teaspoons dried parsley** and season with **salt and pepper**. Mix with your hands, then tip the potatoes into the air fryer and spread out. Air fry at 190°C/380°F for 20 minutes, or until fork tender and almost crispy.

One of our favourite go-to air fryer sides is veggie chips/fries. We will gather root vegetables from the fridge, then prep and cook in the same way as regular chips. This works best with similar cook time root veggies such as beetroot, swede/rutabaga, carrots, parsnips and turnips.

1 swede/rutabaga
2 large parsnips
4 medium carrots
2 tbsp extra virgin olive oil
1½ tsp dried parsley
Salt and black pepper

# crispy root vegetable chips

SERVES **2**   PREP **10 MINUTES**   COOK TIME **30 MINUTES**   CALORIES **340**

**01** Peel the root vegetables and slice them into chips. Aim for a universal size so that they cook evenly.

**02** Put the veggie chips into a mixing bowl, add the olive oil and parsley, and season with salt and pepper. Mix the ingredients well with your hands so that the chips are evenly coated.

**03** Load the veggie chips into the air fryer basket and spread out. Air fry at 160°C/320°F for 25 minutes. Give them a shake, then increase the temperature to 200°C/400°F and cook for another 5 minutes, or until crispy to your liking.

## Love Carrots!

You can also air fry just the carrots. Swap a rainbow of root veggies for just six large carrots and cook following the same time and temperature.

## Seasoning Swaps

Whilst we normally make chips with oregano, you can swap out the dried oregano for any favourite dried seasoning. Swap like-for-like quantities and experiment with seasonings such as peri peri, Cajun, jerk, curry powder or any other personal favourite.

## Make Chips a Meal

You can also make your chips the pairing for a great air fryer meal. Serve chips with steak (see page 72), sausages, frozen fish fingers (see page 25), burgers (see page 80), or another mealtime favourite.

The secret to success is to understand the cooking times of your meal. Let's use frozen fish fingers (fish sticks) as an example: fish fingers take 12 minutes in the air fryer and chips take 25 minutes.

You therefore need to air fry the chips at 180°C/360°F for 13 minutes, first following our chips guide, then shake and move them to the left and add your fish fingers. After a further 12 minute air fry at the same temperature, your fish fingers and chips reach cooked perfection at the same time.

## Quick Loaded Fries

Tip your just-cooked air fryer chips into a silicone baking pan with handles and spoon **hot Bolognese sauce** (see page 84) over the chips. Sprinkle with **125g/4oz/1½ cups grated Cheddar cheese** and air fry at 180°C/360°F for 5 minutes before serving.

## Simple Cheesy Chips

Or if you just want them cheesy, sprinkle **125g/4oz/1¼ cups of grated Cheddar cheese** over the just-cooked chips. Air fry 180°C/360°F for 3 minutes to melt the cheese.

# quick dipping sauces

Below are our two go-to dipping sauces that we often make to serve with our chips, jacket potatoes, breaded chicken and so many other air fryer recipes. Make some extra and store in the fridge for the next time you're air frying.

## quick aioli

When living in Portugal we loved a quick trip over the border into Spain (it was a 90-minute drive) to binge on our favourite Spanish food and plenty of tapas. One favourite is aioli and when we can't get it in Spain, we make plenty of it at home and store it in the fridge for our air fryer potato recipes.

SERVES **4**
PREP **5 MINUTES**
CALORIES **236**

6 tbsp mayonnaise, or more to taste
1 tsp lemon juice
1 tsp garlic purée, or more to taste
1 tsp dried parsley

**01** Combine all the ingredients in a bowl and mix with a fork.

**02** Adjust with extra garlic if not garlicky enough. Or extra mayonnaise if too garlicky.

## sour cream & bacon dip

Another favourite dip we make ahead for our potatoes is sour cream and bacon. Air fry bacon first until super crispy, then add it to a bowl with sour cream and chives – it's so delicious that I can't stop eating it!

SERVES **4**
PREP **3 MINUTES**
COOK **16 MINUTES**
CALORIES **103**

2 streaky bacon rashers/slices
120ml/4fl oz/½ cup sour cream
1 tsp dried chives
Salt and black pepper

**01** Place the bacon into the air fryer basket and air fry at 180ºC/360ºF for 8 minutes. Turn the bacon with tongs and cook for another 8 minutes, or until super crispy.

**02** Allow to cool, then place the crispy bacon slices into a food bag and crush by bashing them with a rolling pin.

**03** Combine the bacon crumbs with the sour cream and chives in a bowl. Season with salt and pepper and mix with a fork.

# everyday potato slices

We call these potatoes our everyday potato slices because they have so many uses. They can be placed over a stew to make a hotpot (as pictured opposite), combined with leftover cheese sauce to make a potato gratin (see page 136), or just kept simple and served as your favourite potato side dish.

......................................

SERVES **4**
PREP **8 MINUTES**
COOK TIME **25 MINUTES**
CALORIES **302**

......................................

6 medium white potatoes
1 tbsp extra virgin olive oil
1 heaped tbsp dried mixed
  herbs/Italian seasoning
Extra virgin olive oil spray
Salt and black pepper

**01** Scrub the potatoes, then thinly slice them into 5mm/¼ inch thick slices, keeping the skin on.

**02** Put the sliced potatoes in a mixing bowl, add the olive oil and mixed herbs and season with salt and pepper. Give everything a very good mix with your hands to make sure the slices are well coated.

**03** Load the potatoes into the air fryer basket and spread out. Air fry at 180ºC/360ºF for 20 minutes, giving them a shake after 10 minutes to stop them sticking together.

**04** When the air fryer beeps, shake again and spray the slices with olive oil to stop them getting dry and help them crisp up. Cook for a final 5 minutes, or until crispy around the edges.

**Make your potato slices into a slow cooker hotpot!** When we are making a hotpot in the slow cooker, we hate the fact that we can't get the sliced potatoes crispy. The air fryer becomes our solution – and is our most used recipe for the sliced potatoes.

Towards the end of the stew's cooking time, we air fry sliced potatoes, as the recipe above, and serve them over the hotpot.

# sour cream & onion cheesy potato skins

If there is a potato recipe worth making the effort for, then it is potato skins.

You air fry the potatoes first, scoop out the centre and mix with sour cream and onion dip as well as plenty of cheese. Add extra cheese on top and air fry until perfectly melted and you will not be able to stop at one.

SERVES **4**
PREP **10 MINUTES**
COOK TIME **48 MINUTES**
CALORIES **352**

4 medium baking potatoes
1 tbsp extra virgin olive oil
Salt and black pepper

**FOR THE POTATO SKINS FILLING**
4 spring onions/scallions, finely chopped
2 tbsp Sour Cream and Bacon Dip (see page 133)
115g/4oz/1¼ cups grated Cheddar cheese, plus extra for sprinkling on top

**01** Scrub the potatoes and prick with a fork several times to allow them to breathe. Spray them with olive oil and sprinkle with salt and pepper, then place the potatoes into the air fryer basket.

**02** Air fry the potatoes at 180ºC/360ºF for about 40 minutes, depending on size, or until fork tender but not overly mushy.

**03** Slice the potatoes in half lengthways, then scrape the potato flesh into a bowl, being careful not to break the skins. Add the spring onions, sour cream dip and grated cheese to the bowl and season with salt and pepper. Mix well with a fork.

**04** Spoon the mixture back into the potato skins and place the loaded skins back into the air fryer basket. Sprinkle the tops with a little extra grated cheese.

**05** Air fry the potato skins at the same temperature for a further 8 minutes, or until the cheese has melted and the filling is piping hot throughout.

# sergio's garlic potatoes with bacon

It was Dom's birthday and we had just moved to Portugal. My parents arrived and said that we were off to the best local restaurant. They introduced us to steak on the stone and the best garlic potatoes we had ever tried. Because it was the best meal on the menu, we returned many times during our 13 years living there and we would often see Sergio prepping the potatoes as we arrived.

It became my mission to recreate those garlic potatoes for the air fryer, and Dom always says that they taste as good as the real thing, just with less oil. Now, when we miss our old Portuguese food, we will make these garlic and bacon potatoes for dinner and serve them, with the fillet steak on page 72.

........................................

SERVES **4**
PREP **10 MINUTES**
COOK TIME **23 MINUTES**
CALORIES **564**

........................................

10 medium red potatoes
1½ tbsp extra virgin olive oil
2 tbsp dried parsley
1 tbsp garlic purée
10 streaky bacon rashers/slices
Salt and black pepper

**01** Peel the red potatoes and cut them into medium cubes. Put them in a bowl with the olive oil, parsley and garlic purée and season with salt and pepper. Mix well with your hands so that the potato cubes are evenly coated.

**02** Tip the garlic potatoes into the air fryer basket and air fry at 180ºC/360ºF for 12 minutes, or until almost fork tender and starting to brown.

**03** While the potatoes are cooking, cut the bacon into squares. When the air fryer beeps, give the potatoes a shake and scatter the bacon over the potatoes. Air fry at the same temperature for a further 6 minutes.

**04** Shake the potatoes and use a spatula to mix the bacon into the potatoes. Increase the temperature to 200ºC/400ºF and air fry for a final 5 minutes, or until the potatoes and bacon are nice and crispy.

**Prefer Parmentier potatoes?** Start cooking the potatoes in the same way as above, cooking for 12 minutes. Meanwhile, make a garlic butter. Add **2 tablespoons softened butter**, **1 teaspoon dried parsley** and **2 teaspoons garlic purée** to a small bowl and mix well. Skip the bacon and toss the almost cooked potatoes in the garlic butter instead. Load the potatoes back into the air fryer and cook for a final 6 minutes at 200ºC/400ºF, or until crispy to your liking.

# easy cajun potato wedges

**Did you know, these potato wedges were the first recipe we ever shared on RecipeThis? They have been a firm fan favourite ever since 2015. They are easy to prep, taste amazing and we have them often on a Saturday night.**

SERVES **4**
PREP **6 MINUTES**
COOK TIME **20 MINUTES**
CALORIES **272**

5 medium white potatoes
1 tbsp extra virgin olive oil
2 heaped tbsp Cajun seasoning
Extra virgin olive oil spray
Salt and black pepper
Sour cream, to serve (optional)

**01** Scrub the potatoes and cut them in half lengthways, then slice each half into wedges to get roughly 8 wedges per potato. Put them in a mixing bowl with the olive oil and Cajun seasoning. Season with salt and pepper and mix well with your hands so that the wedges are evenly coated.

**02** Load the wedges into the air fryer basket and spread out. Air fry at 180ºC/360ºF for 15 minutes, then give them a shake and cook for a further 5 minutes at the same temperature.

**03** Shake the potato wedges and do a fork test to make sure they are fork tender. Spray the wedges with olive oil, increase the temperature to 200ºC/400ºF and cook for a final 5 minutes, or until crispy and golden before serving.

# the ultimate air fryer jacket potato bar

People are amused when we say we take our air fryer on holiday with us. We then point out that we use it for the easiest recipes to save ourselves money. When they ask "What is your top travel recipe?", we always answer with a jacket potato bar, or what you might call baked potatoes. If you have not heard of a jacket potato bar before, it's simply a potato buffet. You bake potatoes in the air fryer, then serve them with a mix of leftovers, as well as traditional toppings.

If we know we will be travelling, we will cook extra at mealtimes and freeze the leftovers, and these will become our baked potato bar main bowls. Here are a few suggestions from recipes in the cookbook:

- Bolognese (page 84)
- Accidental Mushroom Stroganoff (page 121)
- Sour Cream & Bacon Dip (page 133)
- Quick Aioli (page 133)
- Avocado Crema (page 120)

Then have some little pots filled with grated cheese, coleslaw, salsa, butter and, of course, baked beans.

You can also make more if feeding more people, or scale it down to feed just two.

SERVES **4**
PREP **10 MINUTES**
COOK TIME **45 MINUTES**
CALORIES **187 (SEE BELOW)**

.................................................

4 medium baking potatoes
Extra virgin olive oil spray
Salt and black pepper
a small bowl each of grated Cheddar cheese, coleslaw, salsa, baked beans
1 recipe quantity each of Bolognese (page 84) and Sour Cream & Bacon Dip (page 133)
Various leftovers (optional)
4 tbsp salted butter

.................................................

**01** Scrub the potatoes and prick them with a fork so that they can breathe.

**02** Place them on a clean chopping board and spray on all sides with olive oil, then sprinkle all over with salt and pepper.

**03** Place the potatoes in the air fryer basket and air fry at 180°C/360°F for 45 minutes, or until fork tender and crispy.

**04** Once cooked, place the potatoes on a serving board and serve with the cheese, coleslaw, salsa, beans, bolognese, sour cream dip, any leftovers you need to use up – and let's not forget about the butter.

**Note** If your potatoes are large, they will need 50–60 minutes to cook.

**Calorie counting?** As all these potato fillings are flexible, the calories stated above are for the potato only (based on an average 175g/6oz baking potato). Do refer to specific recipes for the calorie counts of suggested fillings.

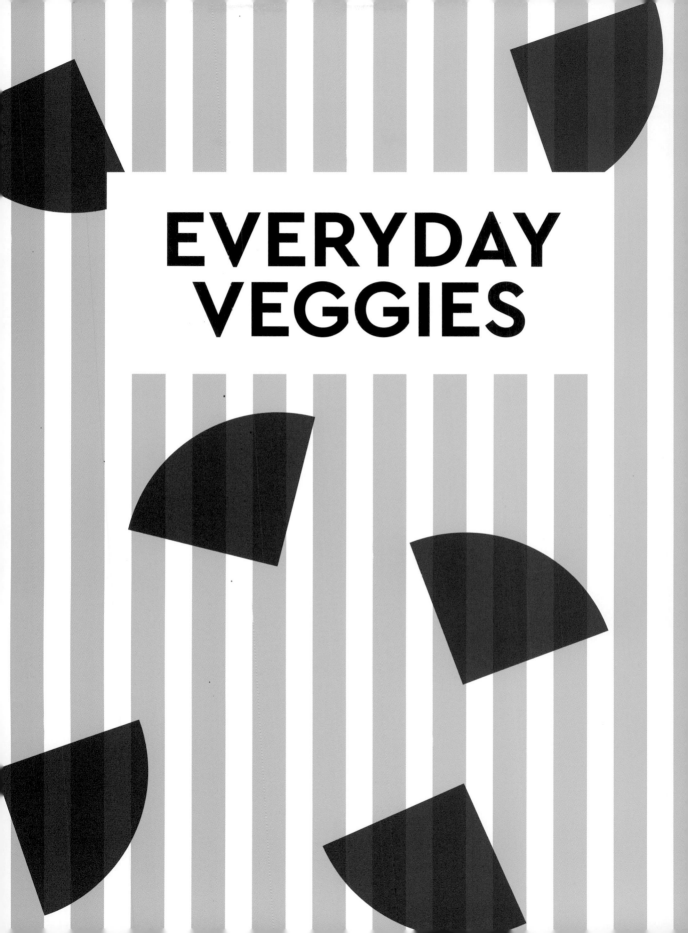

# EVERYDAY VEGGIES

# let's air fry veggies

Roast your veggies in the air fryer and you will never want to return to the oven method again. The vegetables cook much faster, don't require a preheat, keep their great flavour and, best of all, require very little oil.

Master one recipe for vegetables and you will find you can mix and match the same technique with many different vegetables.

First we are going to share with you our favourite method to air fry cubed vegetables. Then you can repeat with other veggies thanks to our vegetable cooking times list (page 150) and variety of recipes in this chapter.

# uncomplicated butternut squash

Let us show you an example from the vegetable cooking times list. Butternut squash is one of the most delicious and easiest air fryer veggies and easy to swap for other winter squash. Master the technique of squash cubes, then try the same method with similar veggies.

450g/1lb (prepared weight) peeled and diced butternut squash
2 tsp extra virgin olive oil
1 tsp dried parsley
Salt and black pepper

SERVES **2**   PREP **5 MINUTES**   COOK TIME **20 MINUTES**   CALORIES **134**

**01** Put the cubed butternut squash into a mixing bowl. Add the olive oil and dried parsley and season with salt and pepper. Mix well with your hands.

**02** Tip the squash into the air fryer and air fry at 180ºC/360ºF for 20 minutes, or until fork tender and starting to crisp.

## Top Tips

**Butternut squash healthy swaps** It was during our introduction to Paleo in 2015 that we first became butternut squash fans. We soon swapped potatoes for squash. You can do the same and make butternut squash fries using our veggie fries recipe on page 130, or why not use squash for roast potatoes on page 170?

**Use pumpkin instead** Butternut squash can also be swapped for pumpkin. When we go pumpkin picking we always buy extra, then cube in bulk and enjoy lots of air fryer cubed pumpkin.

# air fryer vegetable cooking times

Load 450g/1lb of the listed veggies into a bowl with 2 teaspoons of extra virgin olive oil and 1 teaspoon of your favourite dried seasonings. Mix well with your hands and load into the air fryer.

**Aubergine/eggplant** 180°C/360°F – 14 minutes

**Frozen baby carrots** 170°C/340°F – 25 minutes

**Corn on the cob** 180°C/360°F – 15 minutes

**Baby corn** 180°C/360°F – 12 minutes

**Pak choi/bok choy** 180°C/360°F – 6 minutes

**Cherry tomatoes** 180°C/360°F – 4 minutes

**Courgette/zucchini** 180°C/360°F – 12 minutes

**Sliced (bell) peppers/capsicum** 180°C/360°F – 10 minutes

**Sliced onion** 200°C/400°F – 8 minutes

**Radishes** 180°C/360°F – 18 minutes

**Cubed pumpkin or butternut squash** 180°C/360°F – 20 minutes

**Sliced carrots** 180°C/360°F – 15 minutes

**Halved Brussels sprouts** 180°C/360°F – 10 minutes

**Cabbage steaks** 160°C/320°F – 20 minutes

**Beetroot wedges** 180°C/360°F – 20 minutes

**Frozen broccoli** 170°C/340°F – 20 minutes

**Fresh broccoli** 160°C/320°F – 15 minutes

**Fresh cauliflower** 160°C/320°F – 20 minutes

---

When shopping for vegetables, you will often find bags of prepared ones reduced in price because they have a short shelf life. These are perfect for loading into the air fryer the same day.

We recommend the Mediterranean bags that usually contain prepped courgette/zucchini, red onion and red peppers, and sometimes garlic and cherry tomatoes too. These are quicker to prep and cook than root vegetables, making them perfect for busy weeknight dinners.

450g/1lb prepared
  Mediterranean vegetables
1 tbsp extra virgin olive oil
½ tsp dried basil
½ tsp dried oregano
Salt and black pepper

# quick mediterranean vegetables

SERVES **2**   PREP **2 MINUTES**   COOK TIME **21 MINUTES**   CALORIES **190**

**01** Put the vegetables into a mixing bowl. Add the olive oil to the bowl along with the dried herbs, then season with salt and pepper. Mix well with your hands. Remove any cherry tomatoes – if they are included – and set aside, as they will need a shorter cooking time.

**02** Tip the Mediterranean vegetables into the air fryer basket and air fry at 160°C/320°F for 16 minutes.

**03** Shake the veggies and add the cherry tomatoes to the fryer now, if using. Cook for a final 5 minutes at 180°C/360°F, or until the tomatoes have softened and the rest of the veg are crispy.

**Tip** You can experiment with other veggie bags, for example a root veg casserole mix with carrots, baby potatoes and turnip. Follow the same method but cook at 180°C/360°F for 25 minutes in total.

# easy peasy cheesy asparagus

This reader's favourite is the fastest cooking air fryer veggie, takes just seconds to prep and tastes even better loaded with melted cheese. Delicious paired with our quick aioli from page 133.

..............................

SERVES **2**
PREP **2 MINUTES**
COOK TIME **10 MINUTES**
CALORIES **162**

..............................

225g/8oz asparagus spears
Extra virgin olive oil spray
2 tsp butter
28g/1oz/⅓ cup grated
  Parmesan cheese
Salt and black pepper

**01** Trim the woody bottoms off the asparagus spears and season with salt and pepper.

**02** Place the asparagus into the air fryer basket making sure that the spears all lay flat, then spray with olive oil. Air fry at 180°C/360°F for 8 minutes, or until the asparagus is fork tender.

**03** Remove the asparagus and add a layer of foil to the air fryer basket, then place the asparagus back in the basket on top of the foil. Scatter small pieces of butter over the asparagus, then sprinkle with the grated cheese.

**04** Air fry at 200°C/400°F for a further 2 minutes to melt the cheese before serving.

# garlic butter mushrooms with rosemary

Garlic mushrooms are another simple but delicious air fryer veggie. Button mushrooms are cooked with fresh garlic and rosemary to flavour them, and are then tossed in melted butter.

.................................

SERVES **2**
PREP **6 MINUTES**
COOK TIME **9 MINUTES**
CALORIES **109**

.................................

225g/8oz button mushrooms
½ tsp garlic powder
6 garlic cloves
4 fresh rosemary sprigs
Extra virgin olive oil spray
2 tsp melted butter
Salt and black pepper

**01** Place the mushrooms on a chopping board and slice in half (or keep whole if small). Season the mushrooms with the garlic powder and salt and pepper.

**02** Peel the garlic cloves.

**03** Put the mushrooms, garlic cloves and rosemary sprigs into the air fryer basket and spray everything with olive oil. Air fry at 180ºC/360ºF for 6 minutes.

**04** Remove the rosemary from the air fryer and spray the mushrooms again with olive oil. Increase the heat to 200ºC/400ºF and cook for a further 3 minutes, or until the mushrooms have a nice colour and have shrunk. Discard the garlic cloves.

**05** Put the melted butter into your serving dish, add the mushrooms and stir to fully coat them in the butter before serving.

**Tip** You can melt butter in the air fryer. Simply put it in a ramekin dish and air fry at 120ºC/250ºF for 2–4 minutes, depending on the quantity.

In the Milner house we love garlic and add it to a lot of our favourite recipes. But who wants to spend time peeling and sautéing garlic? Instead you can cook garlic ahead of time in the air fryer (without having to peel the cloves) and store it in the fridge for when you need garlic purée in a recipe.

Simply roast the garlic in the air fryer, then squeeze the sweet, caramelised cloves out of the skins and they are ready to use.

3 medium garlic bulbs
Extra virgin olive oil spray
1 tsp dried basil
Salt and black pepper

# no-peel roasted garlic

MAKES **3**   PREP **2 MINUTES**   COOK TIME **25 MINUTES**   CALORIES **7**

**01** Chop the tops off the garlic bulbs to expose the top of the cloves.

**02** Place the garlic bulbs onto a sheet of foil, spray with olive oil and sprinkle with the basil, then season with salt and pepper. Wrap the garlic in foil and place the parcel into the air fryer basket.

**03** Air fry the garlic at 180ºC/360ºF for 15 minutes, then loosen the foil at the top to expose the top of the garlic.

**04** Air fry at the same temperature for a further 10 minutes, or until the garlic cloves are fork tender. Remove the foil parcel from the air fryer and let the garlic bulbs cool.

**05** Once cool enough to handle, one by one pick up the garlic bulbs, hold them upside down and squeeze out the garlic cloves onto a plate. Store in an airtight container in the fridge until ready to use.

**Using your roast garlic** Many of the recipes in this book use garlic purée and you can replace the purée with this roasted garlic in any of them. Why not try it in the tandoori chicken (page 60), meatballs (page 86), salmon bowls (page 98), vegetarian lasagne (page 116) or for Sergio's potatoes (page 141)?

Looking for a healthy evening snack in front of the TV? Then nothing beats a quick bowl of kale chips. One bag of curly kale will fill a bowl for a quick and easy snack.

85g/3oz curly kale
1 tbsp extra virgin olive oil
1 heaped tsp dried mixed herbs
Salt and black pepper

# a bowl of kale chips

SERVES **2**   PREP **5 MINUTES**   COOK TIME **5 MINUTES**   CALORIES **23**

**01** Remove the stems from the kale and rip into large pieces. Put them in a mixing bowl, add the olive oil and herbs and season with salt and pepper. Mix well with your hands until the kale is well coated in all the seasonings and oil.

**02** Load the kale into the air fryer basket and cook at 180ºC/360ºF for 3 minutes. Shake the air fryer, then increase the heat and cook at 200ºC/400ºF for a final 2 minutes, or until you have crispy kale chips. Tip into a serving bowl and enjoy.

# week-night honey glazed carrots

When we bought our house in Portugal, our kind neighbour Maria gave us a large jar of honey as a housewarming gift. It was the start of a honey addiction (especially for Jorge) and now we can't cook carrots without glazing them in honey. These honey carrots are ridiculously simple, making them ideal for hectic weeknights.

SERVES **2**
PREP **10 MINUTES**
COOK TIME **35 MINUTES**
CALORIES **252**

6 large carrots
1 tbsp extra virgin olive oil
1 heaped tsp dried thyme
1 tbsp clear honey
Salt and black pepper

**01** Peel the carrots and slice them into large chunks on the diagonal. Put the carrot chunks in a bowl with the olive oil and dried thyme. Season with salt and pepper and mix well, then load the carrots into the air fryer basket.

**02** Air fry the carrots at 160ºC/320ºF for 25 minutes, then increase the temperature to 180ºC/360ºF and cook for a further 5 minutes, or until fork tender.

**03** Transfer the carrots back to the bowl and add the honey. Mix with a spoon to fully coat the carrots with honey, then tip the carrots back into the air fryer basket.

**04** Air fry the glazed carrots at 200ºC/400ºF for a final 5 minutes before serving.

**Swaps** Instead of carrots, you can make this recipe with parsnips. Or for a festive side dish, why not do half carrots and half parsnips?

# courgette pizza slices

Whether you call it courgette or zucchini, it makes perfect veggie pizza slices – my favourite use for courgette in the summer months. Courgette slices form little pizza bases, which are loaded up with cheese and a sprinkle of oregano.

SERVES **2**
PREP **5 MINUTES**
COOK TIME **11 MINUTES**
CALORIES **167**

½ medium courgette/zucchini
Extra virgin olive oil spray
4 tsp dried oregano
3 tbsp light cream cheese
28g/1oz/⅓ cup grated
  Cheddar cheese
Salt and black pepper

**01** Slice the courgettes into 6mm/¼in thick slices (I usually get around 12 slices from a medium courgette) and spray the tops with olive oil. Sprinkle with half the dried oregano and season with salt and pepper.

**02** Place the slices in the air fryer, spreading them out so that none are on top of each other. Air fry at 180ºC/360ºF for 8 minutes, or until soft in the middle and starting to get crispy.

**03** Remove the courgette slices and spread them with cream cheese. Sprinkle with grated cheese and press it down into the cream cheese so that it doesn't fly away, then finish by sprinkling over the remaining oregano.

**04** Return the courgette slices to the air fryer and cook at 200ºC/400ºF for a final 3 minutes to melt the cheese.

# crispy frozen cauliflower

When the kids are at school on busy weekdays, Dom and I will have salmon and cauliflower for lunch. Both will cook from frozen so there's zero food waste (you are only getting out what you need) and we can take a healthy lunch from frozen to our plates with hardly any prep. You can find our frozen salmon recipe on page 90.

........................................

SERVES **2**
PRE **5 MINUTES**
COOK TIME **20 MINUTES**
CALORIES **219**

........................................

675g/1½lb frozen cauliflower
  florets
2 tsp sweet smoked paprika
1 tsp chilli flakes/red pepper
  flakes
1 tbsp extra virgin olive oil
1 tbsp balsamic vinegar
Salt and black pepper

**01** Place the frozen cauliflower florets into the air fryer basket, spreading them out so that they cook evenly. Air fry at 160ªC/320ºF for 15 minutes.

**02** Meanwhile, put the paprika, chilli flakes, olive oil and balsamic vinegar in a large bowl and mix together to form a paste.

**03** When the air fryer beeps, tip the cauliflower into the bowl with the marinade, season with salt and pepper and stir to coat well.

**04** Tip the cauliflower back into the air fryer basket. Increase the heat to 190ºC/380ºF and cook the cauliflower for a further 5 minutes, or until the cauliflower is crispy to your liking, before serving.

**Tip** Aim to use cauliflower florets that are similar in size, otherwise you will get overcooked smaller bits and undercooked large florets.

**Add more flavour** Cauliflower is great for absorbing flavours. Try the spice mix in the main recipe, or experiment with one of the below:

- **Salt & pepper:** On busy weekdays, Dom and I just spray the florets with **olive oil** and season with **salt and pepper**.
- **Cajun:** We love to serve cauliflower with our Cajun potato wedges from page 143 and fillet steak from page 72. Just spray **olive oil** over the cauliflower and sprinkle with **1 tablespoon of Cajun rub**.
- **Honey & garlic:** The same sticky honey and garlic marinade we make for our chicken thighs on page 56 also makes a delicious flavour for cauliflower. Mix the **honey** and **garlic** in a bowl in the same way we do in the recipe above.

If Sofia and Jorge could choose one side dish that they love the most, it would be frozen corn on the cob cooked in the air fryer. Not only does it taste fantastic, but its simple preparation makes it perfect for busy weeknights. (Pictured on page 81.)

...................................................

4 mini frozen corn on the cobs/ corn cobettes
4 tsp butter
Salt and black pepper

# sofia & jorge's corn on the cob

MAKES **4**   PREP **4 MINUTES**   COOK TIME **15 MINUTES**   CALORIES **99**
...................................................

**01** Load the corn cobs into the air fryer basket and cook at 180ºC/360ºF for 12 minutes, or until fork tender.

**02** Create an open parcel of foil in the shape of your air fryer basket. Our air fryer is square shaped, therefore we made a square parcel. Add the corn on the cob to the foil and place the foil into the air fryer basket.

**03** Season the corn with salt and pepper, then spread a teaspoon of butter over each piece of corn.

**04** Increase the heat to 200ºC/400ºF and cook for 3 minutes more.

**05** Roll the corn in any melted butter that has collected in the foil and serve.

**Tip** The greatest thing about using a layer of foil is that it makes it easy to move your food out of the air fryer without burning yourself – and also makes cleaning the air fryer easier.

Not in the mood for peeling and chopping veggies for dinner? Then let us introduce you to no-prep air fryer green beans. Serve them with air fryer salmon (see page 90) or air fryer chicken breast (page 50) for a healthy dinner.

...................................................

450g/1lb frozen trimmed green beans
1 tsp butter
Salt and black pepper

# lazy green beans

SERVES **2**   PREP **1 MINUTE**   COOK TIME **8–14 MINUTES**   CALORIES **102**
...................................................

**01** Put the frozen green beans into the air fryer basket. Season with salt and pepper.

**02** Air fry at 180ºC/360ºF for 8 minutes, or until warmed through. If you like the green beans crispy – more like veggie chips – add 6 more minutes to the cooking time.

**03** Serve with a little butter added on top and it will melt from the heat of the green beans.

Brussels sprouts are one of those foods you either love or hate. Whilst our kids roll their eyes at the thought of having to eat a single sprout, Dom and I would have them for lunch every day, given the opportunity. But because they are not always in season, and they can take a while to prepare, we love cooking frozen sprouts in the air fryer.

......................................

450g/1lb frozen Brussels
  sprouts
1 tsp extra virgin olive oil
1 heaped tsp mixed dried
  herbs/Italian seasoning
2 tbsp chopped bacon
Salt and black pepper

# the best frozen sprouts & bacon

SERVES **2**   PREP **2 MINUTES**   COOK TIME **13 MINUTES**   CALORIES **193**

**01** Put the frozen sprouts into a mixing bowl and add the olive oil and dried herbs. Season with salt and pepper and mix well with your hands.

**02** Load the sprouts into the air fryer basket and cook at 180ºC/360ºF for 8 minutes.

**03** Add the bacon bits and mix with a spatula, then cook at the same temperature for 5 more minutes, or until the sprouts and bacon are crispy.

Growing up, our grandparents had everything with peas. Pie and peas, pork chops and peas, lamb chops and peas, and the list went on. I'm sure it was because peas were cheap and easy. With the air fryer you don't need to boil a pan of peas. You can simply grab some peas from the freezer, toss them in seasoning and butter, and air fry.

......................................

225g/8oz/1¾ cups frozen
  garden peas
2 tsp dried parsley
2 tsp dried mint
1 tsp extra virgin olive oil
1 tsp butter
Salt and black pepper

# quick buttered peas

SERVES **2**   PREP **2 MINUTES**   COOK TIME **8 MINUTES**   CALORIES **150**

**01** Put the frozen peas in a mixing bowl and add the dried herbs and olive oil. Season with salt and pepper and mix well.

**02** Tip the frozen peas into the air fryer basket and cook at 180ºC/360ºF for 5 minutes, or until piping hot.

**03** When the air fryer beeps, transfer the peas to a silicone pan. Chop the butter into small chunks and scatter them over the peas.

**04** Put the silicone pan with the peas back into the air fryer basket. Increase the heat to 200ºC/400ºF and air fry for a further 3 minutes until the butter is melted. Stir and then serve.

# THE ULTIMATE ROAST DINNER

# Let's air fry a roast dinner

We were driving home from Christmas shopping last year and listening to the radio, hoping for Christmas songs. The radio host came on and said he could never do a Christmas dinner in the air fryer because he would need six air fryers. Dom and I were shell shocked and it stayed in our memories. We have cooked many Christmases, Easters, Thanksgivings and other celebrations, along with Sunday roasts, all in the one air fryer.

We see it as the ultimate air fryer challenge and, once mastered, is a stress-free way to cook special dinners with plenty of sides. We have also included some extra seasonal sides to get you in the festive spirit.

## roast dinner times and temperatures

We love to play a game called "beat the oven". On the packaging of meat, you will see a time guide for cooking in the oven; we love the idea of halving it and creating a full roast dinner in half the time.

Talking about the time... The time for the average roast in the air fryer is 45 minutes to 1 hour, versus 1½ to 1¾ hours for the oven.

You can achieve an all-in-one roast in less time by making use of all the space in the air fryer. Fill the gaps around the meat with your sides, then remove and replace items so that it can all be ready at the same time. You also have the time that the roast meat is resting to be able to finish your sides and bring everything together on the dinner table. Firstly, let's put the roast dinner menu together.

## choosing the meat

We recommend you start your roast dinner plan by choosing the meat. You can use any roasting meats that you would normally cook in the oven, but they need to be small enough to fit in the air fryer. This would, of course, rule out a whole turkey, but you can cook a turkey crown (also known as a bone-in turkey breast), or a smaller part of the bird, such as a turkey thigh or drumstick.

**Chicken or duck** will fit well in the air fryer. We love to collect the duck fat from the bottom of the air fryer and use it for duck fat potatoes.

**Lamb** is also a good option; we love either a lamb shoulder or a boneless leg joint.

**Pork** is amazing roasted in the air fryer. Whilst developing recipes for this cookbook, we did pork shoulder, pork loin and a boneless pork leg joint.

**Beef** is also an air fryer favourite of ours, but stick to a classic roasting cut, such as silverside, topside, round roast, rump, rolled brisket or tenderloin; avoid braising or chuck as it is too tough when cooked in the air fryer.

**Gammon**, popular in the UK and perfect for cooking in the air fryer, is simply uncooked ham, and requires the same time and temperature as a pork or lamb roast.

**Three-Bird Roast.** Here in the UK we have a three bird roast which is turkey, duck and chicken, rolled up and wrapped in bacon to make an impressive roast. Because it's similar in shape and size to a boneless roast beef or lamb you can use the same time and temperature.

You can also use the air fryer to **reheat** previously cooked roasts. Perfect for making ahead and taking the stress out of meal times. You can reheat ham, pork, chicken, turkey, lamb or duck. Although, in the interests of food safety, do not reheat meat more than once.

You can also go small and just do quicker cooking sides alongside faster cooking meat such as pheasants, partridges or poussin/Cornish game hens. See my guide to a smaller roast on page 179

# air fryer beef pot roast

A traditional pot roast has three main ingredients: the roast beef, potatoes and carrots. Before we dive into a full chicken dinner, this air fryer version of a pot roast is an easy starting step.

SERVES **4**
PREP **5 MINUTES**
COOK TIME **45 MINUTES–1 HOUR**
CALORIES **878**

1.1kg/2½lb beef topside/top
   round roast
1 tbsp soy sauce
4 tbsp Worcestershire sauce
1 tbsp dried Italian seasoning
4 large carrots
5 medium potatoes
1 tbsp extra virgin olive oil
2 tsp dried rosemary
1 tsp dried thyme
1 tsp dried parsley
Salt and black pepper

**01** Score the meat, then drizzle over the soy sauce and half the Worcestershire sauce and rub in all over. Season the beef with the Italian seasoning and salt and pepper, making sure the seasoning gets into the scored sections.

**02** Put the beef in the air fryer basket and cook at 180°C/360°F for 20 minutes.

**03** While the beef cooks, peel the carrots and potatoes and cut them into quarters. Put them in a bowl and add the rest of the Worcestershire sauce, the olive oil, rosemary, thyme, parsley and a generous sprinkling of salt and pepper.

**04** When the air fryer beeps, add the carrots and potatoes into the gaps in the basket. Cook at the same temperature for a further 25 minutes, at which point it will be rare to medium – add an extra 10 minutes for medium, or an extra 15 minutes for well done.

**05** Allow to rest for 5 minutes, then serve.

**Pot roast swaps** This is a basic recipe you can mix and match. Swap the topside/top round roast for an equal weight of pork, gammon, lamb, venison, prime rib, rolled brisket, or a three-bird roast. Best of all, they can all be cooked at the same time and temperature.

**All about the weight** The roasting meats we have used have been between 1kg/2lb 4oz and 1.4kg/3lb 2oz. We recommend staying within this range, otherwise the meat and veggies won't fit properly. If in the lower weight range, drop the cook time by 8 minutes, and up by 8 minutes for the higher range.

# the essential sides

Now let's talk about the dream sides. What you will love about these sides is that they will easily pair with any of the roasting meat options.

# duck fat roast potatoes

We have enjoyed roast potatoes cooked in the air fryer for 10 years. But it wasn't until five years of cooking roasties the air fryer way that we swapped the olive oil for duck fat. They were so amazing that we now only ever have roasties with duck or goose fat.

But before you tell us off for using a high fat ingredient, note that the air fryer is about reducing fat and still making crispy food. You only need a fraction of duck fat needed to cook them in the oven.

.......................................................

SERVES **4**
PREP **10 MINUTES**
COOK TIME **30–34 MINUTES**
CALORIES **294**

.......................................................

900g/2lb medium red potatoes
1 tbsp duck or goose fat
2 tsp dried rosemary
1 tsp dried thyme
A pinch of mustard powder
Salt and black pepper

**01** Peel the potatoes and cut in half and then half again to create quarters. Put them in a bowl with the duck fat, rosemary, thyme and mustard powder. Season generously with the salt and pepper and mix the potatoes thoroughly with your hands so that they are evenly coated.

**02** Load the potatoes into the air fryer basket and spread out. Air fry at 160ºC/320ºF for 25 minutes, or until the potatoes are fork tender.

**03** Shake the potatoes, then air fry at 200ºC/400ºF for another 5 minutes to crisp them up. If you are not happy with the level of crispness, cook for another 4 minutes, or until they are done to your liking.

**Tip** You can use any potato, although we find we get the best results from red potatoes as they are less starchy and lend themselves to air frying.

What is not to love about pigs in blankets? Mini sausages, good. Crispy bacon, good. Cooked in the air fryer, good. You can prepare them up to three days in advance, then store them on a plate in the fridge and air fry with your roast dinner. Or if you don't cook them all, you can wrap raw pigs in blankets in foil and freeze for later.

4 slices smoked streaky bacon
8 cocktail/mini sausages

# make-ahead pigs in blankets

MAKES **8**   PREP **5 MINUTES**   COOK TIME **10 MINUTES**   CALORIES **52**

**01** Slice the bacon rashers in half widthways to create eight shorter strips of bacon. Wrap each sausage in streaky bacon. Cover and place in the fridge if making ahead.

**02** When you are ready to cook, place the pigs in blankets into the air fryer basket, seam sides down and spread them out.

**03** Air fry at 180°C/360°F for 10 minutes, or until the bacon is ultra crispy and the sausages are piping hot in the centre.

**Make "pigs in a blanket"** In the USA, sausages are wrapped in pastry rather than bacon. To make these, wrap **cocktail/mini sausages** in **puff pastry or crescent roll** and air fry at 180°C/360°F for 12 minutes.

Our favourite side dish to serve with our roast dinner is homemade stuffing. The easiest way to prepare and cook stuffing in the air fryer is by making stuffing balls. It also keeps the cook time shorter.

340g/12oz pork sausage meat
½ medium onion
2 tsp dried mixed herbs/Italian seasoning
2 tsp dried thyme
2 tsp dried parsley
2 large eggs
120g/4¼ oz/2 cups fresh breadcrumbs
Salt and black pepper

# homemade stuffing balls

MAKES **12**   PREP **5 MINUTES**   COOK TIME **10 MINUTES**   CALORIES **141**

**01** Put the sausage meat into a mixing bowl. Peel and finely dice the onion and add it to the bowl with the dried herbs. Season with salt and pepper and mix really well with your hands.

**02** Crack the eggs into the bowl and mix, then gradually add the breadcrumbs until well combined. Divide the mixture into 12 equal portions and roll into balls.

**03** Load the stuffing balls into the air fryer basket, spreading them out. Air fry at 180°C/360°F for 10 minutes, or until they are crispy and piping hot in the centre.

**Can't get sausage meat?** Use plain pork sausages, squeeze the meat out of the skins into the mixing bowl and continue with the recipe as above.

# homemade yorkshire puddings

Both Dom and I were raised, fell in love, and bought our first house in Yorkshire. It's also where Kyle, our first son, was born. When we lived abroad, we made plenty of Yorkshire puddings in the air fryer when we were missing our favourite home comfort food. They never fail, taste amazing, are never doughy and always rise to the occasion!

......................................

MAKES **8**
PREP **5 MINUTES, PLUS RESTING**
COOK TIME **25 MINUTES**
CALORIES **108**

......................................

125g/4½oz/1 cup plain/all-
   purpose flour
1 large egg
240ml/8fl oz/1 cup whole/full-
   fat milk
4 tsp beef dripping
Salt and black pepper

**01** Put the flour in a mixing bowl and season with salt and pepper.

**02** Make a well in the centre of the flour and crack the egg into the well.

**03** Mix the egg with a fork, gradually incorporating the flour around the outside as you go, until all the egg and flour is mixed.

**04** Gradually add the milk, continuing to mix with a fork as you trickle it in. Mix until you have a bubbly, pancake-style batter.

**05** Allow the batter to sit in the mixing bowl for 20 minutes before moving on to the next step. This will help the Yorkshire puddings to rise.

**06** After 10 minutes, divide the beef dripping among eight mini metal pudding tins, putting ½ teaspoon in each, then place the pudding tins into the air fryer basket. Note, you can cook four at a time if you can't fit them all in one go. Air fry at 200ºC/400ºF for 10 minutes to get the tins really hot and the fat sizzling.

**07** When the air fryer beeps, quickly pour the batter into the tins, dividing it equally among the eight tins (or four, if doing in batches). Air fry at the same temperature for another 10 minutes.

**08** On the beep, use tongs to turn over the Yorkshires and air fry at the same temperature for a final 5 minutes, then flip back over with tongs and serve. If you have to repeat the process to cook the remaining four puddings, just heat the dripping in the tins for 5 minutes before adding the batter, as the air fryer will already be really hot.

**Note** It is traditional to make Yorkshire puddings with beef dripping and it makes a big difference to the flavour. However, if you can't source beef dripping, you can swap it for lard or vegetable oil.

**Love frozen Yorkshire puddings?** We love cooking frozen Yorkshire puddings in the air fryer too and they are so crispy and fast. Simply add them to the air fryer and cook at 200ºC/400ºF for 4 minutes.

# the best homemade cornbread

Do you love cornbread but hate cleaning the skillet? The air fryer option makes it much easier as you can cook it in a silicone pan, then it just pops out and the pan only needs a simple wipe clean.

MAKES **12 SLICES**
PREP **8 MINUTES**
COOK TIME **30 MINUTES**
CALORIES **164**

150g/5½oz/1 cup polenta/
    cornmeal
125g/4½oz/1 cup self-raising/
    self-rising flour
240ml/8½fl oz/1 cup buttermilk
2 large eggs
4 tbsp extra virgin olive oil
4 tbsp clear honey

**01** Put the cornmeal and flour in a mixing bowl and mix with a fork.

**02** Add the buttermilk, then crack the eggs into the bowl. Mix again with your fork.

**03** Next, add the oil and honey and continue to mix with a fork.

**04** Add 3 tablespoons of cold water, scrape the edges of the bowl with a spatula and do a final mix with the fork.

**05** Pour the cornbread batter into a 20cm/8inch silicone baking pan and place the pan into the air fryer basket.

**06** Air fry at 180ºC/360ºF for 15 minutes, then reduce the temperature to 170ºC/340ºF and cook for another 15 minutes, or until the thermometer inserted into the centre of the bread comes out clean.

**Making cornbread muffins?** Spoon the mixture into silicone cups instead and air fry at 180ºC/360ºF for 12 minutes.

# the creamiest green bean casserole

One of our favourite veggies to air fry is green beans. They are easy, fast, delicious and you can also cook them for longer as a fries alternative. But the overlooked and even tastier option is to finish cooking the green beans with cheese sauce and crispy bacon and breadcrumbs to create a green bean casserole.

.................. ......................

SERVES **4**
PREP **8 MINUTES**
COOK TIME **30 MINUTES**
CALORIES **301**

.................. ......................

450g/1lb frozen green beans
Extra virgin olive oil spray
1 tbsp dried parsley
1 tsp onion powder
1 tsp garlic powder
3 rashers/slices streaky bacon
840g/1lb 14oz/3½ cups (about ½ recipe quantity) Quick Hidden-Veggie Cheese Sauce (see opposite)
3 tbsp fresh breadcrumbs
Salt and black pepper

**01** Place the green beans in the air fryer basket and air fry at 180ºC/360ºF for 8 minutes until they are piping hot and cooked through.

**02** Spray the green beans with olive oil spray, sprinkle the parsley and onion and garlic powders over them and season with salt and pepper. Cook at 200ºC/400ºF for a further 6 minutes, or until almost crispy. Move the green beans into a silicone pan with handles and put to one side.

**03** Put the bacon slices into the air fryer and air fry at 200ºC/400ºF for 6 minutes, or until crispy. Once cool enough to handle, chop the bacon up into little bits.

**04** Assemble the casserole by pouring the cheese sauce over the green beans in the silicone pan and sprinkle the top with breadcrumbs and then with the bacon bits. Air fry at 200ºC/400ºF for a further 10 minutes, or until the cheese sauce is piping hot.

**Quick Hidden-Veggie Cheese Sauce** We love to make a cheese sauce with air fried butternut squash. It eliminates the butter and flour and makes it healthier.

Put **900g/2lb peeled and cubed butternut squash** into a bowl and add **1 tablespoon dried oregano** and **1 tablespoon extra virgin olive oil**. Season with **salt and pepper** and mix with your hands. Tip into the air fryer and air fry at 180ºC/360ºF for 20 minutes, or until tender.

Put the squash in a blender with **600ml/21fl oz/2½ cups veggie stock**, **1 teaspoon dried basil**, **1 teaspoon dried parsley** and **1 teaspoon garlic puree**, and season with **salt and pepper**. Add **225g/8oz/2⅓ cups grated Cheddar cheese** and **6 tablespoons cream cheese** and blend until smooth.

This cheese sauce recipe will make enough for both the green bean casserole (above) and the potato gratin on page 136, or you can freeze any leftovers.

# the ultimate roast chicken dinner in the air fryer

Now you have mastered the beef roast – and maybe mixed and matched with different boneless meats – and tried some sides, let's aim to make a much bigger roast dinner.

This time we're going to swap beef for a whole chicken, making it even more affordable. But you can swap the chicken for duck, turkey crown or similar bone-in poultry, if you wish.

.............................................

SERVES **4**
PREP **15 MINUTES**
COOK TIME **1 HOUR**
CALORIES **1404**

.............................................

4 medium carrots
4 medium parsnips
2½ tbsp extra virgin olive oil
1 tsp dried thyme
1 medium whole chicken
   (giblets removed)
1 tbsp garlic powder
1 tbsp dried parsley
Make-Ahead Pigs In Blankets
   (prepped from page 171)
Homemade Stuffing Balls
   (prepped from page 171)
Duck Fat Roast Potatoes
   (prepped from page 170)
225g/8oz Brussels sprouts
½ tbsp balsamic vinegar
½ tbsp maple syrup
1 tbsp dried Italian seasoning
1 tbsp clear honey
Salt and black pepper

**01** Peel the carrots and parsnips and slice them into sticks. Put them in a bowl with 1 tablespoon of the olive oil and the thyme, and season with salt and pepper. Toss with your hands until the veggies are all evenly coated with the oil, then load into the air fryer basket.

**02** Put the chicken, breast side down, on a clean chopping board and smoother in ½ tbsp olive oil, and ½ tbsp each of garlic powder and dried parsley. Place the chicken, still breast side down, into the air fryer basket, over the carrots and parsnips. Air fry at 180ºC/360ºF for 25 minutes.

**03** Meanwhile, prepare the pigs in blankets, stuffing balls and roast potatoes, according to the recipes.

**04** When the air fryer beeps, remove the chicken and put to one side. Place the stuffing balls in the air fryer over the carrots and parsnips. Cook at the same temperature for 5 minutes.

**05** Whilst the air fryer is busy, prepare the sprouts. Slice them in half and put in a bowl. Add ½ tablespoon olive oil and the balsamic vinegar, maple syrup and Italian seasoning. Season with salt and pepper and mix well so that they are evenly coated.

**06** When the air fryer beeps, remove the stuffing, carrots and parsnips and put to one side.

**07** Return the chicken to the air fryer, this time breast side up. Season the breast side with the final ½ tablespoon olive oil and the remaining ½ tablespoon each of garlic powder and parsley.

**08** Add the potatoes and sprouts to any available gaps and cook at the same temperature for a further 20 minutes, or until the chicken reads an internal temperature of 70ºC/160ºF or above. Remove the chicken and allow to rest before carving.

**09** In the meantime, add the pigs in blankets to the air fryer and cook with the sprouts and potatoes for 5 minutes.

**10** When the air fryer beeps, remove the sprouts and potatoes and load onto a serving dish.

**11** Put the stuffing balls back in the air fryer basket. Toss the carrots and parsnips in the honey and return them to the air fryer, too. Cook the stuffing, carrots, parsnips and pigs in blankets for a final 5 minutes.

**12** Carve the chicken and serve with the sides. You now have a roast chicken dinner with five sides done in an hour.

# the smaller roast dinner

Our ultimate chicken roast is perfect for a family of four. But what if you are feeding 1–2 people? In this case, you can go small with pheasant, poussin/Cornish game hen, partridge or a very small chicken.

Pheasant or poussin/Cornish game hen cooks in 30 minutes, whilst partridge cooks in 25 minutes. Or keep it simple and cook half a chicken in 25 minutes.

As they are much smaller, you will have a lot more room to fill the air fryer with more sides, making it less effort to balance air fryer times.

## How to Do it Differently

Halve the ingredients for two, or quarter the ingredients if feeding one.

Cook the carrots, parsnips, Brussels sprouts and roast potatoes with the bird at 180ºC/360ºF for 25 minutes.

Remove the sides and add the pigs in blankets and stuffing balls to the air fryer. Cook for 5 minutes, then remove the bird and allow it to rest.

Toss the carrots and parsnips in honey.

Cook the stuffing and pigs in blankets for 7 more minutes along with the carrots and parsnips before serving everything together.

You now have a smaller roasting option, cooked in 37 minutes.

This is also what we recommend making for Christmas dinner in the air fryer for two people, or for one person with some yummy leftovers for the next day.

## Want Gravy?

We love to make gravy from the juices in the bottom of the air fryer. We are going to show you a quick example with juices from our roast chicken so that you understand the method.

Fifteen minutes before the roast is done add a **peeled and sliced onion** to the bottom of the air fryer with the juices and mix with a spatula. After the 15 minutes is up, transfer the juices and the onion to a mixing jug. Our juices made 240ml/8½fl oz/1 cup.

To the juices in the jug, add **360ml/12fl oz/1½ cups chicken stock** and thicken with **1 teaspoon cornflour/cornstarch** (or a spoonful of mashed potatoes). Warm up in the microwave for a minute, then transfer to a gravy boat.

You can use this gravy method with any meat you have cooked in the air fryer. For example, if you have just made a lamb roast, then follow the same method but swap the chicken stock for lamb stock. Or use the same idea with beef, gammon, turkey, duck or pork.

## Want Quick Cranberry Sauce?

Put **85g/3oz fresh cranberries** in a ramekin dish. Sprinkle with **2½ tablespoons granulated sugar**, a **pinch of cinnamon** and **1 teaspoon honey**. Air fry for the final 10 minutes with the remaining sides, making a space in the air fryer for the ramekin. When the air fryer beeps, pulse the cranberry mix with a hand blender, keeping it a little chunky, and serve.

# SAVOURY
# BAKING

# let's bake!

In the Milner kitchen we love to bake in the air fryer. We are starting here with savoury bakes, then walking you through sweet bakes in the next chapter.

You might be wondering what you can bake in the air fryer? Well, think of anything you bake in the oven, but in smaller bakeware and mostly without a preheat; quiches, tarts, flans, pies, even homemade bread or pizza can all be made in the air fryer. You can also use the air fryer for proving the dough.

Bread in the air fryer is fantastic and a great starting point to air fryer savoury baking.

You could take any favourite bread recipe and then use the air fryer instead of the oven. Or why not start by trying our basic bread recipe, then adapt it?

Sofia and Jorge have made many of the baking recipes in this cookbook, meaning that they are so easy that kids can make them. Or why not make these recipes with your kids or grandkids?

# baking accessories

But before we dive into air fryer baking, let's talk about the baking accessories we use the most.

**01** **Loose-based baking pan** We use this metal 20cm/8inch dish for most of our flans, quiches, tarts and pies – including all those in this book. It's small enough to fit in most air fryers with a large basket and, because of the loose bottom, it's so easy to remove your pie or tart from the pan.

**02** **Mini springform cake pans** The kids and I discovered these at baking class and we love the fact that several mini pans will fit in the air fryer at once. We use them for the mini carrot cakes on page 211.

**03** **Silicone bakeware** Silicone is your air fryer best friend. Forget soaking and scrubbing bakeware or lining it with baking parchment.

We love the small cups for muffins, the loaf pans for breads, and the round pans for cakes. We also recommend silicone spatulas to keep your air fryer free from scratches.

**04** **Thermometer** Most associated with testing the temperature of meat, it's also ideal for inserting into cakes to check that they are done. Insert it into the centre of the cake and if it comes out clean, your cake is done. We use a thermometer every time we bake a sponge cake in the air fryer.

# pull-apart bread rolls

We are going to start with bread rolls. These rolls are perfect for sandwiches, soup, or even to wow your guests with at Thanksgiving. A reader favourite for many years, the idea came about because we had lots of bread machine dough and needed a quick way to cook it. Even better, you can use the air fryer as a proving method to help the bread rise quickly, and you don't need to add sugar to the dough.

.................................................

MAKES **8**
PREP **15 MINUTES**
COOK TIME **15 MINUTES, PLUS PROVING**
CALORIES **293**

.................................................

440g/15½oz/3½ cups plain (all-purpose) flour, plus extra for dusting
½ tsp salt
½ tsp black pepper
60g/2¼oz/¼ cup salted butter, softened)
240ml/8½fl oz/1 cup whole/full-fat milk
1 tbsp extra virgin olive oil
2 tsp fast-action dried yeast
1 egg, beaten (optional)

**01** Put the flour, salt, pepper and butter into a mixing bowl. Chop the butter into chunks, then rub it into the flour using your fingertips until the mixture resembles breadcrumbs.

**02** Pour the milk and oil into a jug, mix, then microwave for 30 seconds–1 minute to warm it up. You don't want it too hot or it will kill the yeast – lukewarm is perfect.

**03** Add the yeast to the flour bowl, then gradually add the lukewarm milk and oil, mixing with your hand as you add it, until you have a sticky dough.

**04** Flour a clean worktop and your hands. Tip out the dough and knead for 5 minutes, or until you have a soft bread dough.

**05** Divide the dough into eight equal portions, then shape them into balls.

**06** Load the eight balls into a 20cm/8inch round silicone baking pan, arranging a ring around the outside, with a final one in the centre so that you have no gaps. Once they prove they will expand and join to create a pull apart effect.

**07** Air fry the bread rolls at 75ºC/165ºF for 30 minutes. Once the machine beeps, leave the rolls in the air fryer for a further 30 minutes, or until they have doubled in size. We find that they will have risen to just above the top of the baking pan. What is brilliant is that the heat from the air fryer will prove the rolls without needing to knead and prove again.

**08** Once risen, brush the top of the rolls with egg wash, if using, and air fry at 180ºC/360ºF for 15 minutes, or until golden and firm.

## Make Pull-Apart Garlic Bread

You can add a garlic glaze to your pull-apart bread rolls. Follow the recipe opposite and just modify as follows. After the rolls have proved in the air fryer, place a small bowl into the air fryer basket with **1 tablespoon unsalted butter**, **½ teaspoon dried parsley**, and **1 teaspoon garlic purée**. Cook at 120ºC/250ºF for 4 minutes, or until the butter is fully melted. Stir and put to one side.

Air fry the rolls (without the egg wash) at 180ºC/360ºF for just 12 minutes. When the air fryer beeps, brush the melted garlic butter over the top of the bread, then air fry for the final 3 minutes.

## ... Or Pizza Garlic Breads

You can also make pizza-style garlic breads by using a couple of the balls of the dough recipe opposite. Knead two balls together, then roll them out like a pizza. Brush with a quarter of the **garlic butter** mixture above using a pastry brush. Cook at 180ºC/360ºF for 8 minutes, until risen and golden.

## Love Garlic Baguettes?

We love the small garlic baguettes that we buy when on a weekly food shop. You can cook them in the air fryer for 6 minutes at 170ºC/340ºF.

## Make Mini Loaves

We love the cute little silicone loaf tins you can get for the air fryer. Instead of making bread rolls, you can split the dough between two mini loaf tins. Simply roll the portions into sausage shapes, place in the loaf tins, then prove and cook in the air fryer as we have done for the pull-apart bread.

## Air Fryer Proving Confession

We always forget about our bread and leave it proving for too long in a warm air fryer. It was through this that we realised you could cook something in the air fryer, then place bread in the warm fryer to prove in the residual heat for an hour, and come back to perfectly risen bread dough. You can do the same, or simply air fry at 75ºC/165ºF for 30 minutes.

# thin-crust hawaiian pizza

The problem with cooking pizza in the air fryer is that many pizza bases don't fit the size of your air fryer. Our solution is to thinly roll our bread dough to the size and shape of our air fryer. One batch of dough will make four thin crust pizzas and, even better, you don't need any air fryer accessories because the pizza cooks directly in your air fryer basket. Plus, thin crust pizza in the air fryer is delicious; the base is so crispy and you can make it with so many different pizza toppings. This is one of our favourites.

SERVES **4**
PREP **10 MINUTES**
COOK TIME **10 MINUTES**
CALORIES **746**

Extra virgin olive oil spray
Flour, for dusting
1 recipe quantity bread dough
   (page 184, but see method
   opposite)
4 tbsp tomato pizza sauce
2 tsp tomato purée/tomato
   paste
2 tsp dried oregano
A pinch of garlic powder
4 slices ham, cut into chunks
4 canned pineapple slices, cut
   into chunks
170g/6oz/1½ cups grated
   mozzarella cheese
fresh basil leaves, to serve
   (optional)

**01** Spray the air fryer basket with oil to create a non-stick coating.

**02** Make the pull apart bread dough following the method on page 184, though because you are using it for pizza, we recommend not proving the dough. Divide the dough into four equally-sized balls.

**03** Dust a clean worktop and a rolling pin with flour and roll out one of your dough balls to the shape of your air fryer and to the thickness of a thin pizza crust. Carefully transfer the dough into the air fryer basket.

**04** In a small bowl, combine the tomato sauce, tomato purée, oregano and garlic powder. Spread a quarter of the tomato sauce onto the dough, leaving a 1cm/½ inch border around the edge. Air fry for 4 minutes at 180ºC/360ºF to give the dough a head start.

**05** Slice the ham into chunks and the pineapple slice into eighths. Sprinkle one-quarter of the grated cheese over the pizza, then scatter over one-quarter the ham and pineapple.

**06** Air fry the pizza at 180ºC/360ºF for 6 minutes, or until the ham is starting to crisp at the edges and you have a crispy pizza base. Tilt the air fryer basket over a plate to remove your pizza and serve with a few basil leaves sprinkled over.

**07** Repeat this method until you have four pizzas (or freeze leftover dough and save for later). To speed up the process, we will be rolling out the next pizza whilst the previous one is air frying.

**Sofia & Jorge's deep pan pizza** You can also make the same amount of dough into two deep pan pizzas. Use a 20cm/8inch metal pizza pan for each of the pizzas and roll to your preferred thickness, then cover with favourite toppings. Sofia and Jorge both love theirs with plenty of **mozzarella cheese**, **cherry tomatoes**, as well as some little **spoonfuls of cream cheese**. Air fry at 180ºC/360ºF for 15 minutes and you have perfect pizza.

**Make a naan pizza** Instead of making the dough, spread the topping over **four naan breads** and air fry at 180ºC/360ºF for 6 minutes.

**What about frozen pizza?** You can also cook small frozen pizzas in the air fryer. Load into the air fryer and cook at 180ºC/360ºF for 8 minutes, or until you have a crispy crust and piping hot toppings.

# cheesy scones for everything

I once asked my American cousin what American biscuits were. She put it simply and said that they are cheese scones with buttermilk and loads of salt. Years later, I tried them in the US and she was spot on.

But I had an idea: if I made cheese scones, I could use the dough as a replacement for dumplings over stew or casseroles. I made the family a stew with scones for dinner and it was so good everyone went back for seconds. It is now a reader's favourite.

Now Dom and I make these scones for enjoying halved and spread with butter, for dumplings in stew, or even as a topping for sweet cobbler when we swap the cheese for sugar.

......................................

MAKES **6**
PREP **10 MINUTES**
COOK TIME **8 MINUTES**
CALORIES **214**

......................................

175g/6oz/1⅓ cups self-raising/
  self-rising flour, plus extra for
  dusting
28g/1oz/2 tbsp butter
1 large egg
1 tsp mustard powder
½ tsp garlic powder
2 tsp dried parsley
85g/3oz/1 cup grated Cheddar
  cheese
2 tbsp whole milk/full-fat milk,
  plus extra if needed
Salt and black pepper

**01** Put the flour and butter in a mixing bowl and use your fingertips to rub the fat into the flour. Continue to do this until the mixture resembles coarse breadcrumbs.

**02** Crack the egg into the bowl, add the mustard and garlic powders, parsley and cheese, season with salt and pepper and mix well.

**03** Flour your hands, then add the milk to the bowl and use your hands to bring it together into a big dough ball. Be patient as it can take a few minutes to mix well for a soft dough. If too dry, add a little extra milk.

**04** Tip the dough onto a clean, floured worktop, press down and shape with your hands until you have a round disc that is 1.5cm/½ inch thick, then cut into six equal portions. Roll each portion into a ball, then place the balls in the air fryer, spreading them out so that they are not touching one another.

**05** Air fry the scones at 180ºC/360ºF for 8 minutes, or until you tap the bottom of a scone and it is firm to the touch and makes a hollow sound.

**American biscuits** Looking for traditional biscuits to make biscuits and gravy? Swap the milk for **buttermilk** and add an extra **1 teaspoon sea salt**.

# easy cheesy savoury muffins

We put these cheesy muffins in our top five treats to cook in the air fryer. Inspired by an Aussie pastry chef we met when we lived in Portugal, these cheese muffins are light, and best served warm as the cheese melts. Good for picnics, buffet food, parties, packed lunches and road trips. (Pictured on page 189.)

................................................

MAKES **12**
PREP **10 MINUTES**
COOK TIME **19 MINUTES**
CALORIES **208**

................................................

3 tbsp salted butter, softened
1 tsp garlic purée
1 large egg
180ml/6fl oz/¾ cup whole/full-fat milk
6 tbsp full-fat Greek yoghurt
3 tbsp extra virgin olive oil
1 tsp dried parsley
1 tsp dried mixed herbs/Italian seasoning
¼ tsp mustard powder
190g/6¾oz/1½ cups self-raising/self-rising flour
125g/4½oz/1¼ cups grated mature/sharp Cheddar cheese
4 slices ham, cut into chunks
Salt and black pepper

**01** Put the butter in a small air fryer-safe container with the garlic purée. Air fry at 120ºC/250ºF for 4 minutes to melt the butter.

**02** Crack the egg into a large mixing bowl and add the milk, yoghurt, olive oil, parsley, mixed herbs and mustard powder. Season with salt and pepper, then stir.

**03** Add the melted butter and garlic, then mix well with a fork.

**04** Next, sift in the flour and stir in, then finally stir in the cheese and ham.

**05** Using an ice cream scoop, add a scoop of muffin batter to 12 silicone muffin cups, continuing to fill them until all the batter has been distributed evenly among the cups.

**06** Place the cups into the air fryer basket and cook at 180ºC/360ºF for 15 minutes, or until a thermometer inserted into the centre of a muffin comes out clean.

**Mix and match** Usually we make these muffins with just cheese and leftover ham, but you can swap the ham for bacon bits, sweetcorn, red (bell) peppers, mushrooms or another savoury muffin favourite ingredient.

# easy peasy shortcrust pastry

This is the shortcrust pastry my grandma taught me to make as a kid. She would use it for pies, pasties, flans and so much more. It was easy to adapt for the air fryer and can be used for both sweet and savoury recipes.

Over the holidays, the kids and I will make a big batch and use it in multiple recipes. Plus, you can wrap any leftovers in foil and freeze for later. Use the quantity below to make enough for your recipe – the method is the same for both.

.....................................

MAKES **ENOUGH FOR ONE (20CM/8IN) PIE OR QUICHE – REFER TO QUANTITIES BELOW** PREP **15 MINUTES**

.....................................

**FOR 1 ENCLOSED PIE**
250g/9oz/2 cups plain/all-purpose flour
3 tbsp granulated sugar (for sweet pastry)
125g/4½oz/½ cup butter (salted for savoury/unsalted for sweet)

**FOR 1 OPEN PIE OR QUICHE**
180g/6¼oz/1⅓ cups plain/all-purpose flour
2 tbsp granulated sugar (for sweet pastry)
90g/3¼oz/6 tbsp butter (salted for savoury/unsalted for sweet)

**01** Put the flour in a mixing bowl and add the sugar if you're making sweet pastry. Chop the butter into cubes and add them to the flour. Rub the butter into the flour with your fingertips until the mixture resembles breadcrumbs.

**02** Gradually add a little cold water at a time (approximately 4 tablespoons for the enclosed pie quantity and 3 tablespoons for the open pie or quiche) as you mix the dough until the mixture begins to come together into a soft dough. Transfer the dough to a floured clean worktop and knead briefly until it's nice and smooth.

**03** Roll out the dough and use in a recipe, or wrap in cling film/plastic wrap to save for later. If using later, bring the dough to room temperature before rolling.

# veronica's cheese & ham quiche

Growing up, my favourite party food was my aunt's quiche. It tasted so good and everyone would be talking about it. I had watched her make it many times and it was one of the first things I made for Dom to try and impress him (after a call to my aunt first). Well, it worked! It's his favourite and I will always make it for summer picnics as well as a treat on New Year's Eve.

SERVES **8**
PREP **15 MINUTES**
COOK TIME **25 MINUTES**
CALORIES **311**

Flour, for dusting
1 recipe Easy Peasy Shortcrust Pastry (open pie or quiche quantity – see page 191), at room temperature
½ small onion
4 slices ham
170g/6oz/2 cups grated mature (sharp) Cheddar cheese
3 large eggs
120ml/4fl oz/½ cup whole milk
2 tsp dried parsley
2 plum tomatoes
1 tsp dried basil
Salt and black pepper

**01** Dust a clean worktop and a rolling pin with flour. Roll out the pastry until you have a thin crust for the bottom of your baking pan (see page 182) – there is enough pastry for a 20cm/8inch dish, but you may have to do it in a 18cm/7inch dish if you have a smaller air fryer. We recommend you place the dish over the rolled out pastry to make sure it is large enough to cover the bottom and the sides.

**02** Carefully wrap the pastry around the rolling pin, then transfer it to the dish, unrolling it carefully. Tuck it into the dish with your fingers, making sure that it is smooth, then trim off the extra overhang with a vegetable knife.

**03** Finely dice the onion and cut the ham into chunks. Sprinkle both the onion and ham into the base of the dish, spreading them out evenly. Then sprinkle over the cheese, reserving a little for the top of the quiche.

**04** Crack the eggs into a jug, add the milk and beat with a fork. Add the parsley, season with salt and pepper and mix well.

**05** Pour the egg mixture over the fillings in the pastry case, until the pastry case is three-quarters full. Finely slice the tomatoes and decorate the top with them. Sprinkle over the reserved cheese, then sprinkle with basil.

**06** Place the quiche into the air fryer basket. Air fry at 160ºC/320ºF for 17 minutes, then lower the heat to 150ºC/300ºF and cook for a further 8 minutes, or until the quiche has lost its wobble.

**Make a cheese flan instead!** Did you know that there is only one difference between a simple cheese quiche and a cheese flan?

To make a quiche, the ingredients are added first, then beaten egg is poured over. Whilst to prepare a cheese flan, the ingredients are mixed with the egg for a more structured look.

To make a cheese flan, mix the egg and the milk first, then add the cheese, mix with a fork and pour into the baking dish. Cook for the same time and temperature as a cheese quiche.

# creamy chicken & mushroom pie

We love pie in the air fryer. You can use our shortcrust pastry recipe (or buy it or use a standard pie crust) and make either sweet or savoury pies. You can also use the same pastry recipe for quiche (see page 193). Plus, you can mix and match with other favourite fillings, such as our meat pie on page 82.

........................................

SERVES **4**
PREP **20 MINUTES**
COOK TIME **34 MINUTES**
CALORIES **754**

........................................

Flour, for dusting
1 recipe Easy Peasy Shortcrust Pastry (enclosed pie quantity – see page 191), at room temperature
1 medium onion
225g/8oz button mushrooms
Extra virgin olive oil spray
2 tsp dried parsley
1 large cooked chicken breast
340g/12oz/1½ cups cream cheese
360ml/12fl oz/1½ cups chicken gravy (see page 179 or shop-bought)
1 egg, beaten (optional)
Salt and black pepper

**01** Dust a clean worktop and a rolling pin with flour. Roll out two-thirds of the pastry until you have a thin crust for the bottom of your baking pan (see page 182) – we make a 20cm/8inch pie, but you may have to do it in an 18cm/7inch dish if you have a smaller air fryer. We recommend you place the dish over the rolled out pastry to make sure it is large enough to cover the bottom and the sides.

**02** Carefully wrap the pastry around the rolling pin, then transfer it to the dish, unrolling it carefully. Tuck it into the dish with your fingers, making sure that it is smooth, then trim off the extra overhang with a vegetable knife. Add any offcuts to your remaining pastry for when you roll out for the top of the pie.

**03** Prick the bottom of the pie pastry with a fork to help it breathe as the air circulates around the air fryer. Don't chill because pie crust in the air fryer cooks better from room temperature. Just leave to one side while you prepare the filling.

**04** Next, peel and dice the onion and chop the mushrooms in half, or into quarters if they are big. Load them into the air fryer basket, spray with olive oil and sprinkle with the parsley, then season with salt and pepper. Air fry at 180ºC/360ºF for 6 minutes, or until the mushrooms have softened.

**05** Chop the cooked chicken breast into cubes. Put them in a large bowl and add the cream cheese, gravy, and the cooked onion and mushrooms. Season well with salt and pepper and stir. Pour the pie filling into the dish and spread it out evenly.

**06** Next, roll out the remaining pastry and lay it over the top of the pie. Trim away the overhanging pastry with a vegetable knife and press down around the edge to seal the pastry. Decorate the top of the pie with offcuts, if you like. Brush the top of the pie with egg wash. Pierce a hole in the middle of the pie top so the steam can escape and the pastry won't go soggy.

**07** Carefully place the chicken pie into the air fryer basket and air fry at 180ºC/360ºF for 20 minutes, or until the pie is golden on top.

**Frozen chicken pie** If you have a chicken pie in the freezer, it will take just 20 minutes at 180ºC/360ºF to warm up from frozen.

# SWEET
# TREATS

# Let's air fry a cake

If you have a sweet tooth, you will love baking your favourite sweet treats in the air fryer. From cakes and brownies to sweet pies and muffins, there is a sweet treat for everyone

# the ultimate chocolate cake

Chocolate cake is our favourite cake to cook in the air fryer and it's so easy. We have been making chocolate cake in the air fryer for the last 10 years and whenever there is a birthday cake that needs making, out comes the air fryer cake pans.

First, we're going to share with you the technique of an air fryer cake, and then you can repeat it with any cake that you are craving. We will then run through a quick cake decorating technique for an easy celebration cake.

SERVES **8**
PREP **15 MINUTES**
COOK TIME **1¼ HOURS**
CALORIES **690**

225g/8oz/1 cup unsalted butter, softened
450g/1lb/2¼ cups granulated sugar
3 large eggs
1 tbsp vanilla extract
1½ tbsp extra virgin olive oil
50g/1¾oz/½ cup cocoa powder
600ml/21fl oz/2½ cups skimmed/fat-free milk
400g/14oz/3 cups self-raising/self-rising flour

**01** Put the butter and sugar in a mixing bowl and, using an electric hand mixer, beat until it changes colour and becomes almost white and fluffy in texture. Crack the eggs into the bowl, add the vanilla and olive oil, and mix again with your hand mixer until smooth and creamy.

**02** Once it is creamy, add the cocoa powder and milk and mix until you have a wonderfully creamy chocolate batter. Gradually add the flour, mixing with a wooden spoon as you go until combined. Divide the cake batter evenly between two silicone 20cm/8inch cake pans and smooth out the tops with a wooden spoon.

**03** Cook the cakes one at a time. Air fry the first one at 180°C/360°F for 10 minutes, then adjust the temperature to 160°C/320°F and cook for a further 25 minutes to allow the centre to cook and not just create a crust. The chocolate cake is cooked when a thermometer inserted into the centre of the cake comes out clean. If not fully set, cook at 150°C/300°F for a further 10 minutes.

**04** Remove the cake from the air fryer and peel away the silicone pan. Repeat the process to cook your second cake. Leave them on a cooling rack to cool completely before decorating.

## Top Tips

**Cook on a low heat** It is essential that you cook on a low heat, otherwise your cake will burn on top and won't be cooked in the centre. Some air fryers are much slower at cooking cake. If this is yours, cook it for another 10 minutes at 150°C/300°F.

**Silicone makes it easy** Avoid scrubbing a cake pan or lining with baking parchment and use silicone cake pans instead. The cake will peel away from the silicone without making any mess.

# rocky road chocolate cake

We make this chocolate cake for family birthdays the most, but it also doubles up brilliantly as a fun cake to make with Halloween leftovers.

Start with some air fryer dark chocolate ganache and then make a mountain of trick or treat leftovers, add melted chocolate and grated chocolate for the ultimate chocolate cake.

..................................................

SERVES **8**
PREP **45 MINUTES, PLUS MAKING THE CAKE**
COOK TIME **10 MINUTES**
CALORIES **1493**

..................................................

1 recipe Ultimate Chocolate Cake (page 198)
80g/2¾oz chocolate chip cookies
60g/2¼oz various chocolate sweets/candy, such as mini chocolate cups and chocolate malt balls
1 tbsp each blonde chocolate chips, fudge pieces and white chocolate buttons
28g/1oz mini pink and white marshmallows
40g/1½oz white chocolate squares
28g/1oz dark (bittersweet) chocolate squares

## FOR THE GANACHE ICING
540g/1lb 3oz dark chocolate
420ml/14½fl oz/1¾ cups double/heavy cream

**01** To make the ganache, break the chocolate into squares and place them into a round silicone pan. Pour over half the cream and air fry at 120ºC/250ºF for 4 minutes.

**02** Stir with a silicone spatula, then add half the remaining cream and air fry for a further 3 minutes. Add the remaining cream and stir until you have a chocolate sauce.

**03** Place the silicone pan onto a cool plate and gently place the plate in the fridge for 30 minutes to cool. Once cool, use an electric hand mixer, on medium speed, to whisk for 3 minutes, or until the ganache is the consistency of whipped cream.

**04** With a bread knife, carefully level one of the cakes and place it onto a cake board. Spread a generous layer of the whipped ganache over the cake, going right to the edges, then place the second sponge on top.

**05** Spread the remaining ganache over the top of the cake, again pushing it right out to the edges to create a lovely swirl around the edge.

**06** Break up the chocolate cookies into varying sized bits and pile them into the middle of the cake. Scatter over your chocolates fudge pieces, chocolate buttons and marshmallows to create a rocky road mountain.

**07** Next, break the white chocolate into chunks, place them into a silicone pan and air fry at 120ºC/250ºF for 3 minutes, or until melted. Mix with a teaspoon, then use the spoon to drizzle the white chocolate over the mountain of chocolate.

**08** Grate the dark chocolate squares over the cake before serving.

**Mix and match** This rocky road cake also works well with Easter and Christmas leftovers, or for a cupboard clear out when making a celebration cake.

# dom's victoria sponge cake

Dom's favourite cake to make in the air fryer is a Victoria sponge or as us Brits call it, a Victoria sandwich cake. Vanilla sponge cake is sliced in half and then a layer of jam and cream is added, and the two half sponges are sandwiched back together.

SERVES **8**
PREP **15 MINUTES**
COOK TIME **35 MINUTES**
CALORIES **648**

230g/8oz/1 cup unsalted butter, softened
250g/9oz/1¼ cups granulated sugar
5 large eggs
2 tbsp vanilla extract
2 tbsp extra virgin olive oil
8 tbsp whole/full-fat milk
225g/8oz/1¾ cups self-raising/self-rising flour

## FOR THE FILLING
180ml/6fl oz/¾ cup double/heavy or whipping cream
2 tbsp strawberry jam/preserve
icing/confectioner's sugar, for dusting

**01** Put the butter and sugar in a mixing bowl and, using an electric hand mixer, beat until it changes colour and becomes almost white and fluffy in texture.

**02** Crack the eggs into the bowl, add the vanilla, olive oil and milk, and mix again slowly with your hand mixer until smooth and creamy.

**03** Slowly add the flour to the batter, mixing with the hand mixer as you add it. Don't over mix because you want a light cake.

**04** Pour the cake batter into an 20cm/8inch silicone cake pan and smooth out the top with a wooden spoon.

**05** Air fry the cake at 160ºC/320ºF for 20 minutes, then cover the top of the pan with foil to stop the cake browning too much. Decrease the temperature to 150ºC/300ºF and cook for a further 15 minutes, or until a thermometer inserted into the centre of the cake comes out clean.

**06** Remove the cake from the air fryer and peel away the silicone pan. Leave the cake on a cooling rack to cool completely before decorating.

**07** Once the cake is completely cool, put the cream in a bowl and whisk with a hand mixer to soft peaks.

**08** Slice the cake in half horizontally with a bread knife and spread the base half with the strawberry jam. Spread the whipped cream over the jam, then sandwich with the top sponge. Dust the top of the cake with icing sugar to finish. Because of the cream, the cake will be need to be stored in the fridge.

**Vary the flavour** You can use this Victoria sponge cake as your master recipe, then mix and match the flavours.

- **Lemon cake:** Swap the vanilla extract for **4 tablespoons lemon juice** and the **finely grated zest of 1 lemon**.
- **Orange cake:** Swap the vanilla extract for **4 tablespoons orange juice** and the **finely grated zest of 1 orange**.
- **Coloured cake:** Make it a fun cake with the kids and add **a few drops of food colouring**.

# sweet pie (three ways)

In our Savoury Baking chapter, we showed you how to make pastry and turn it into a quiche and a chicken and mushroom pie. We are continuing the theme here with three sweet pies: apple, cherry and pumpkin. You can then mix and match with other favourite fillings.

## warm apple pie

**When I was a kid, my dad loved homemade apple pie with custard. As a grown-up, it was the first pie Dom and I converted to the air fryer because it was the easiest to experiment with.**

SERVES **8**
PREP **15 MINUTES**
COOK TIME **28 MINUTES**
CALORIES **493**

Flour, for dusting
1 recipe sweet Easy Peasy
  Shortcrust Pastry (enclosed
  pie quantity – see page 191),
  at room temperature
6 Pink Lady apples
2 tsp lemon juice
1 tsp ground cinnamon
1 tsp grated nutmeg
1 tsp mixed spice/apple-pie
  spice
1 tsp extra virgin olive oil
300g/10½oz sweetened
  condensed milk
2 tbsp Greek yoghurt
1 egg, beaten (optional)
Granulated sugar, for sprinkling

**01** Dust a clean worktop and a rolling pin with flour. Roll out two-thirds of the pastry until you have a thin crust for the bottom of your baking pan (see tip, page 206). We recommend you place the pan over the rolled-out pastry to make sure it is large enough to cover the base and sides.

**02** Carefully wrap the pastry around the rolling pin and transfer it to the baking pan, unrolling it carefully. Tuck it into the pan with your fingers, making sure it is smooth, then trim off the extra overhang with a vegetable knife. Add any offcuts to your remaining pastry for when you roll out the top.

**03** Prick the bottom of the pie pastry with a fork to help it breathe as the air circulates around the air fryer. Don't chill because pie crust in the air fryer cooks better from room temperature. Just leave to one side while you prepare the filling.

**04** Next peel, core and dice the apples and put the chunks into a bowl. Add the lemon juice, dried spices, and olive oil and mix well.

**05** Load the mixture into the air fryer basket and air fry at 180ºC/360ºF for 8 minutes, or until the apples have softened.

**06** Tip the cooked apples into a bowl and add the condensed milk and yoghurt. Mix well, then pour into your lined baking pan and spread evenly.

**07** Next, roll out the remaining pastry and use the rolling pin to lift the pastry and lay it over the top of the pie. Trim away the overhanging pastry with a vegetable knife, then press down around the edge to seal the pastry. Brush the top of the pie with egg wash, then sprinkle the top with sugar. Pierce a hole in the middle of the pie top so that the steam can escape and the pastry won't go soggy.

**08** Place the pie into the air fryer basket and air fry at 180ºC/360ºF for 20 minutes, or until the pie is golden on top.

# mr baker's cherry pie

This cherry pie recipe is dedicated to our late friend and long-time Recipe This reader, who passed away whilst we were developing the recipes for the cookbook. His last request was for a cherry pie all to himself, so it is our honour to make this in his memory. (Pictured on page 207)

.............................................

SERVES **8**
PREP **10 MINUTES**
COOK TIME **20 MINUTES**
CALORIES **324**

.............................................

Flour, for dusting
1 recipe sweet Easy Peasy Shortcrust Pastry (enclosed pie quantity – see page 191), at room temperature
1 × 425g/15oz can cherries, drained
1 tbsp vanilla extract
28g/1oz/2½ tbsp granulated sugar
125g/4½oz/½ cup cherry jam/ preserve
1 egg, beaten (optional)

**01** Dust a clean worktop and a rolling pin with flour. Roll out two-thirds of the pastry until you have a thin crust for the bottom of your baking pan (see tip, page 206). We recommend you place the pan over the rolled-out pastry to make sure it is large enough to cover the base and sides.

**02** Carefully wrap the pastry around the rolling pin and transfer it to the baking pan, unrolling it carefully. Tuck it into the pan with your fingers, making sure it is smooth, then trim off the extra overhang with a vegetable knife. Add any offcuts to your remaining pastry for when you roll out for the top of the pie.

**03** Prick the bottom of the pie pastry with a fork to help it breathe as the air circulates around the air fryer. Don't chill because pie crust in the air fryer cooks better from room temperature. Just leave to one side while you prepare the filling.

**04** Put the drained cherries into a bowl, add the vanilla and sugar and stir well. Gradually stir in the jam, a bit at a time until well mixed and creamy. Pour the cherry filling into your lined baking pan, spreading it out evenly. Don't make the mistake of adding more jam as it will turn to syrup and make your cherry pie watery.

**05** Next, roll out the remaining pastry and lay it over the top of the pie. Trim away the overhanging pastry with a vegetable knife, then press down around the edge to seal the pastry. Brush the top of the pie with egg wash, then pierce a hole in the middle of the pie top so that the steam can escape and the pastry won't go soggy.

**06** Place the pie into the air fryer basket and air fry at 180ºC/360ºF for 20 minutes, or until the pie is golden on top.

**Tip** You can swap the canned cherries for fresh or (defrosted) frozen pitted cherries. If using fresh, cook them first in a ramekin at 180ºC/360ºF for 8 minutes.

# make-ahead pumpkin pie

We first made pumpkin pie in the air fryer for Thanksgiving 2012. It was delicious and started a new Thanksgiving air fryer tradition. Now it's a reader favourite at RecipeThis and many make it ahead to take out the stress of Thanksgiving.

........................................

SERVES **8**
PREP **15 MINUTES**
COOK TIME **20 MINUTES**
CALORIES **351**

........................................

Flour, for dusting
1 recipe sweet Easy Peasy
    Shortcrust Pastry (open pie or
    quiche quantity – see page
    191), at room temperature
½ X 425g/15oz can pumpkin
    purée
2 large eggs
100g/3½oz/½ cup soft light
    brown sugar
3 tbsp granulated sugar
120ml/4¼fl oz/½ cup double/
    heavy cream
2 tsp pumpkin spice
2 tsp ground cinnamon
1 tsp grated nutmeg

**01** Dust a clean worktop and a rolling pin with flour. Roll out the pastry until you have a thin crust for the bottom of your baking pan (see below). We recommend you place the pan over the rolled-out pastry to make sure it is large enough to cover the base and sides.

**02** Carefully wrap the pastry around the rolling pin and transfer it to the baking pan, unrolling it carefully. Tuck it into the pan with your fingers, making sure it is smooth, then trim off the extra overhang with a vegetable knife.

**03** Prick the bottom of the pie pastry with a fork to help it breathe as the air circulates around the air fryer. Don't chill because pie crust in the air fryer cooks better from room temperature. Just leave to one side while you prepare the filling.

**04** Put the pumpkin puree, eggs and sugars in a mixing bowl. Mix with an electric hand mixer until you have a creamy texture. Add the cream and all the dried spices and continue to mix until smooth.

**05** Pour the pumpkin filling into your lined baking pan, spreading out evenly with a spatula so that it looks neat and cooks evenly.

**06** Place the pie carefully into the air fryer basket and air fry at 180°C/360°F for 20 minutes, or until the pie crust is golden and the filling has only a slight wobble. Chill in the fridge overnight before slicing and serving.

**Tip** You can make homemade pumpkin purée by steaming plain pumpkin with a pressure cooker or microwave then drain out the excess liquid. Once cool, it's ready to be used to make pumpkin pie.

**What pie dish to use?** With air fryers of different sizes, you may be wondering what size pie dish to use. We use our 20cm/8inch baking pan/quiche dish which has a loose base (see page 182), making it perfect for pies. But we have an extra large air fryer; if you have smaller one you may need to use a 18cm/7inch dish. Or if you have less space in your fryer, you can always use mini springform pans (see page 182).

# eggless chocolate chip cookies

A reader once asked us if we could make them some cookies without egg as they have an egg allergy. We found this fascinating because the cookie recipe we have followed for decades doesn't have eggs. They taste delicious and Jorge is the first to lick the bowl.

.........................................

MAKES **12**
PREP **10 MINUTES**
COOK TIME **8 MINUTES PER BATCH**
CALORIES **324**

.........................................

160g/5½oz/⅔ cup unsalted butter, softened
100g/3½oz/½ cup soft light brown sugar
50g/1¾oz/¼ cup granulated sugar
4 tbsp honey or maple syrup
3 tbsp whole/full-fat milk
2 tsp vanilla extract
280g/10oz/2¼ cups self-raising/self-rising flour
55g/2oz milk chocolate chunks
100g/3½oz chocolate chips (any colour, or a mixture of colours)

**01** Put the butter and sugars in a mixing bowl and, using an electric hand mixer, beat until it changes colour and becomes almost white and fluffy in texture.

**02** Add the honey or syrup, milk and vanilla and mix in well with the electric hand mixer, then gradually add the flour.

**03** Finish the cookie dough by adding the chocolate chunks and chips and mixing with a silicone spatula.

**04** Divide the dough into 12 portions, then use a cookie scoop or ice cream scoop to make into cookie balls. Line the air fryer basket with foil, then place a few of the cookies inside, allowing space around them for them to spread – you will need to cook them in batches. Air fry at 180°C/360°F for 8 minutes, or until pale golden on top and crisping up around the edges.

**05** Remove the cookies from the air fryer by the foil and allow to cool for 5 minutes to set before serving. Repeat to cook the remaining cookies.

**Chocolate chip swaps** We love to mix and match with our cookies depending on what ingredients we have in – you can do the same. Use white chocolate, dark chocolate, milk chocolate or your favourite chopped chocolate bar, or why not use the leftovers from Easter, Halloween or Christmas?

# coffee-shop chocolate chip muffins

We love making chocolate muffins in the air fryer – they must be loaded with chocolate chips and cocoa for the ultimate chocolate fix. They are cooked in silicone cups for easy washing up, and they are fantastic for picnics or parties.

MAKES **8**
PREP **10 MINUTES**
COOK TIME **15 MINUTES**
CALORIES **325**

1 large egg
80ml/2½fl oz/⅓ cup single cream/half and half
4 tbsp extra virgin olive oil
4 tbsp whole/full-fat milk
1 tsp vanilla extract
28g/1oz/⅓ cup cocoa powder
130g/4½oz/⅔ cup granulated sugar
125g/4½oz/1 cup self-raising/self-rising flour
150g/5½oz chocolate chips (any colour, or a mixture of colours)

**01** Crack the egg into a mixing bowl and add the cream, oil, milk and vanilla. Whisk with an electric hand whisk to combine, then add the cocoa powder and sugar and whisk again.

**02** Now discard the whisk as your mixture will get too thick. Add the flour and mix well with a silicone spatula until everything is combined. Finally stir in the chocolate chips.

**03** Divide the batter among eight silicone cups, making sure they are full to the brim for that coffee-shop muffin look.

**04** Load the silicone cups into the air fryer basket and air fry at 180ºC/360ºF for 15 minutes, or until firm and crispy on top.

**05** Eat warm, or you can place them in an airtight container once cool or store in the fridge.

**Tip** The cream adds to the light fluffy texture of the muffins, but you have choices: you can also use Greek yoghurt, coconut cream for a dairy-free option, sour cream, or our Christmas favourite – brandy cream.

You can add any chocolate you like to the muffins. We added a mix of white, milk and dark chocolate chips, but you can also use bags of chocolate chunks or break up chocolate bars into chunks.

# mini carrot cakes

We have been making carrot cake in the air fryer for many years and it's become an Easter air fryer tradition. But sometimes you want to enjoy cake in a small portion. This recipe will perfectly split between two mini springform pans and because it's smaller, it is quicker to cook than a standard air fryer cake.

SERVES **4**
PREP **15 MINUTES**
COOK TIME **20 MINUTES**
CALORIES **478**

Extra virgin olive oil spray, for greasing
1 large carrot
125g/4½oz/1 cup self-raising/self-rising flour, plus extra for the pan
1 tsp mixed spice/apple-pie spice
1 tsp ground cinnamon
1 tsp ground ginger
¼ tsp ground nutmeg
100g/3½oz/½ cup light soft brown sugar
50g/1¾oz/¼ cup granulated sugar
1 large egg
85ml/2¾fl oz/⅓ cup extra virgin olive oil
1 tbsp whole/full-fat milk

**01** Start by preparing two mini springform cake pans. First spray them with extra virgin olive oil and rub it around the bottom and sides with your fingers. Then dust with a little flour, tapping the bottom of the pan to get the flour to evenly coat the pan.

**02** Peel and grate the carrot. Put it in a mixing bowl and add the flour, all the dried spices and the sugars and mix with a fork.

**03** Make a well in the centre of the mixture and crack in the egg. Add the oil to the well too, then mix well with a fork.

**04** Add the milk to the carrot batter and do a final stir. Pour the cake batter into the prepared pans and place them into the air fryer basket.

**05** Air fry at 180°C/360°F for 15 minutes, then reduce the temperature to 160°C/320°F and cook for a further 5 minutes, or until a thermometer inserted into the centre of a cake comes out clean.

**06** Serve the cakes warm with custard or ice cream.

**Tip** You can swap all the ground spices above for 3¼ teaspoons pumpkin spice, if that's what you have.

# self-saucing chocolate orange pudding

We love self-saucing puddings. You add extra liquid to the cake mix before it cooks and, once air fried, you'll find a hidden chocolate sauce.

You can also mix it up with chocolate chips, chunks of a favourite chocolate bar or, as we have, with chocolate orange segments.

........................................

SERVES **2**
PREP **10 MINUTES**
COOK TIME **14 MINUTES**
CALORIES **678**

........................................

28g/1oz/2 tbsp unsalted butter
70g/2½oz/½ cup self-raising/
  self-rising flour
3¼ tbsp granulated sugar
2 tbsp cocoa powder
Finely grated zest and
  squeezed juice of 1 medium
  orange
1 large egg
3 tbsp whole/full-fat milk
1 tbsp vanilla extract
6 chocolate orange segments
  (such as Terry's)
Vanilla ice cream, to serve
  (optional)

## FOR THE CHOCOLATE SAUCE
5 tbsp boiling water
50g/1¾oz/¼ cup light soft
  brown sugar
1 tsp cocoa powder

**01** Grab two ceramic dishes that will fit the air fryer basket together and distribute the butter between the two. Place in the air fryer and air fry at 120°C/250°F for 4 minutes, or until melted.

**02** Tip the melted butter into a mixing bowl, then smear any butter that's left in the dishes around the bases and sides to grease them.

**03** To the bowl with the butter, add the flour, sugar, cocoa powder, and the orange zest and juice. Mix well with a wooden spoon. Crack in the egg and add the milk and vanilla and stir.

**04** Divide the batter equally between the two dishes. Break the chocolate orange segments into thirds and place them over the cake batter, dividing them equally between the two dishes.

**05** Next, make the sauce. Mix together the boiling water, brown sugar and cocoa powder. Pour half the sauce into each dish, pouring it over the back of a spoon so that it goes in gently and doesn't dislodge your chocolate segments.

**06** Place both dishes into the air fryer basket and air fry at 180°C/360°F for 10 minutes, or until the pudding is firm and crispy on top. Remove from the air fryer and serve immediately, with ice cream, while the middle is still gooey.

# 10-minute blueberry crumble pots

I have loved fruit crumble since my school dinner days. However, warm fruit is not Dom's thing, so I love to make little crumble pots just for me and the kids. The blueberries turn almost to jam and the addition of an oaty crunch makes them taste even better.

.....................................

SERVES **4**
PREP **10 MINUTES**
COOK TIME **10 MINUTES**
CALORIES **375**

.....................................

255g/9oz/2 cups fresh
  blueberries
5 tbsp granulated sugar, plus
  4 tsp for the blueberries
4 tsp maple syrup
125g/4½oz/1 cup self-raising/
  self-rising flour
60g/2oz/¼ cup unsalted
  butter, softened
28g/1oz/⅓ cup porridge oats/
  oatmeal

**01** Divide the blueberries evenly among four ramekins. Sprinkle a teaspoon of sugar and drizzle a teaspoon of maple syrup into each ramekin.

**02** Put the ramekins in the air fryer basket and air fry the blueberries at 180ºC/360ºF for 5 minutes.

**03** In the meantime, put the 5 tablepoons of sugar, the flour and butter into a bowl. Rub the fat into the flour and sugar using your fingertips until the mixture resembles breadcrumbs. Add the oats and stir with a fork until well mixed.

**04** When the air fryer beeps, sprinkle the crumble over the berries, dividing it equally among the four ramekins.

**05** Air fry at 200ºC/400ºF for 5 minutes, or until the blueberries are bubbling and the crumble topping is firm and golden.

# kitty's rock cakes

Whilst most people might associate rock cakes with Harry Potter, my first memory of rock cakes is 15 years before the movies, making them with my Grandma Kitty. We would do lots of baking, both savoury and sweet, then use a bit of everything leftover to make rock cakes, as they are often made from whatever leftover dried fruit you have. You can do any mix of dried peel, raisins and cherries – or my favourite is adding dried cranberries over the Christmas holidays.

........................................

SERVES **8**
PREP **15 MINUTES**
COOK TIME **10 MINUTES PER BATCH**
CALORIES **324**

........................................

225g/8oz/1¾ cups self-raising/
  self-rising flour
100g/3½oz/½ cup granulated
  sugar
115g/4oz/½ cup unsalted
  butter, softened
1 medium egg
115g/4oz/heaped ¾ cup raisins
28g/1oz/¼ cup mixed peel/
  candied peel
4 tbsp whole/full-fat milk
Butter and jam/jelly, to serve
  (optional)

**01** Put the flour and sugar into a mixing bowl and add the butter, chopping it into chunks as you add it. Rub the fat into the flour and sugar with your fingertips until the mixture resembles breadcrumbs, then add the egg, raisins and mixed peel and mix well.

**02** Next, add enough milk to make a wet dough – we recommend adding it a little at a time until you have a dough that is like an overly sticky scone mix.

**03** Line your air fryer basket with foil. Use a tablespoon to add mounds of the batter into the basket – using 2 heaped tablespoons of the mixture per cake – spacing them out so that they have room to spread during cooking. You may have to cook them in two batches – we cook four at a time in our air fryer.

**04** Air fry the rock cakes at 180ºC/360ºF for 10 minutes, or until firm on touch. Repeat to cook the second batch, if you need to.

**05** Serve the rock cakes warm with butter and jam, or allow them to cool on a cooling rack and store in an airtight container for up to 4 days.

# uncomplicated one-pan fudge brownies

When we are craving brownies we want something fast and uncomplicated that will get rid of the craving. What we hate about most brownie recipes is that you melt stuff in the pan, then have one bowl for wet ingredients and one for dry. Instead, we show you how to do it all in one silicone baking pan.

..............................................

MAKES **10**
PREP **8 MINUTES**
COOK TIME **29 MINUTES**
CALORIES **379**

..............................................

75g/2½oz/⅓ cup unsalted
    butter
4 tbsp milk chocolate chips
2 large eggs
1 tbsp clear honey
2 tsp vanilla extract
100g/3½oz/½ cup granulated
    sugar
100g/3½oz/½ cup soft light
    brown sugar
28g/1oz/⅓ cup cocoa powder
65g/2¼oz/½ cup self-raising/
    self-rising flour
4 tbsp dark chocolate chips
4 tbsp white chocolate chips

**01** Put the butter and milk chocolate chips into a round 20cm/ 8 inch silicone pan. Place it into the air fryer basket and air fry at 120ºC/250ºF for 4 minutes to melt the butter and chocolate.

**02** When the air fryer beeps, remove the pan and add the eggs, honey, vanilla and sugars. Mix with a whisk in the silicone pan until it is well combined and thick. Add the cocoa powder, flour and the remaining chocolate chips and mix well.

**03** Place the pan back into the air fryer basket and air fry at 180ºC/360ºF for 15 minutes. Decrease the heat to 160ºC/320ºF and cook for a further 10 minutes, or until a thermometer inserted into the centre of the brownie comes out clean.

**04** Allow the brownies to sit in the pan for 10 minutes to partly cool and set, then slice into portions before serving.

**05** The brownies last for 10 seconds in our house, but if you have more willpower, they will keep in an airtight container for up to 4 days.

# air fryer menus

Now we have shown you lots of different air fryer recipes, let's combine them to make some delicious air fryer meals – from daily themes to make mealtimes less boring, to seasonal menus for special occasions.

## Meatless Monday

- Perfect Halloumi Fajitas (page 112)
- Parmentier Potatoes (page 141)
- Quick Aioli (page 133)

## Taco Tuesday Night

- Taco Tuesday Prawn Tacos (page 103)
- Easy Cajun Potato Wedges (page 143)
- Sour Cream & Bacon Dip (page 133)

## Healthy Wednesday

- Super-Easy Tuna Niçoise (page 100)
- Uncomplicated Butternut Squash (page 148)

## Throwback Thursday

- Uncle Bob's Easy Meatloaf (page 83)
- Duck Fat Roast Potatoes (page 170)
- Week-Night Honey Glazed Carrots (page 156)
- Kitty's Rock Cakes (page 216)

## Friday Fakeaway

- Dom's Easy Cheeseburgers (page 80)
- Sweet Potato Chips (page 130)
- Sofia & Jorge's Corn on the Cob (page 162)
- Sour Cream & Bacon Dip (page 133)

## Pasta Saturday

- The Best Vegetarian Lasagne (page 116)
- Easy Peasy Cheesy Asparagus (page 152)
- Garlic Bread (page 185)

## Stress-free Sunday

- Roast Chicken & Stuffing (page 48)
- Duck Fat Roast Potatoes (page 170)
- Honey-Glazed Carrots (page 156)
- Crispy Frozen Cauliflower (page 160) with Quick Hidden-Veggie Cheese Sauce (page 175)
- Make-Ahead Pigs in Blankets (page 171)
- Gravy (page 179)

## Perfect for Leftovers

- Superhero Hidden-Veggie Burgers (page 118)
- Secret-Ingredient Meatballs (page 86)
- Garlic Bread (page 185)
- Courgette Pizza Slices (page 159)

## Girly Night In

- Simple Scallops Wrapped in Bacon (page 105)
- The Ultimate Air Fryer Jacket Potato Bar (page 144)
- 10-minute Blueberry Crumble Pots (page 214)

## Date Night In

- Steak & Chips (page 72)
- Garlic Butter Mushrooms with Rosemary (page 154)
- Self-Saucing Chocolate Orange Pudding (page 212)

## Games Night

- Sour Cream & Onion Cheesy Potato Skins (page 138)
- Game Night Frozen Wings (page 21)
- Sofia & Jorge's Corn on the Cob (page 162)
- Courgette Pizza Slices (page 159)

## Movie Night

- 10-minute Air Fryer Hot Dogs (page 80)
- Crispy Curried Chickpeas (page 124)
- 10-minute Blueberry Crumble Pots (page 214)

## Summer BBQ Sides

- Seriously Satisfying Vegan Cobb Salad (page 110)
- Devilled Eggs (page 29)
- Jacket Potatoes (page 144)
- Sofia & Jorge's Corn on the Cob (page 162)
- Quick Aioli (page 133)

## Picnic in the Park

- Veronica's Cheese & Ham Quiche (page 193)
- Veggie-Loaded Egg Cups (page 32)
- Super-Easy Tuna Niçoise (page 100)
- Three-Ingredient Cajun Tortilla Chips (page 125)
- Uncomplicated One-Pan Fudge Brownies (page 217)

## Easter Sunday

- Boneless Lamb Roast (see pages 166 and 168)
- Duck Fat Roast Potatoes (page 170)
- Honey Glazed Carrots (page 156)
- The Best Frozen Sprouts & Bacon (page 163)
- Mini Carrot Cakes (page 211)

## Thanksgiving Feast

- Bone-in turkey breast (see pages 166 and 176)
- Duck Fat Roast Potatoes (page 170)
- Seriously Satisfying Potato Gratin (page 136)
- The Creamiest Green Bean Casserole (page 175)
- Pull-Apart Bread Rolls (page 184)
- The Best Homemade Cornbread (page 174)
- Homemade Stuffing Balls (page 171)
- Honey Glazed Carrots & Parsnips (page 156)
- The Best Frozen Sprouts & Bacon (page 163)
- Make-Ahead Pumpkin Pie (page 206)

# index

# thank you

The first thank you goes to *Philips* for bringing the first air fryer to the market in 2010. Without them believing in the air fryer concept, we wouldn't be air frying every day.

To our agent *Clare* who saw our passion for the air fryer and believed in us. Along with *Denise* and *Nicky* at Quarto for holding our hand every step of the way and making it a reality. A special thank you to Becci, our editor, who made us think outside the box and make every recipe into something extraordinary.

To *Sofia* and *Jorge*, our mini authors, for giving up your Christmas holidays to stand beside us in the kitchen and test all the recipes of this cookbook. We loved watching you weigh out ingredients and cover us and yourselves in flour. You're our most critical recipe testers and we love you for your true honesty and passion for the air fryer.

To *Kyle*, our eldest son, for helping us grow RecipeThis and the endless hours you have put into our graphics and videos. We are so proud of what you have become.

To *Sarah* and *Tracy* for all your efforts in the recipe testing process, for giving us a different air fryer point of view, and for being by our side and giving us love and support and hugs when we needed it.

Thank you to the wonderful *readers of Recipe This* for your amazing support, great friendship and telling us what air fryer recipes make your life easier so that we can create better recipes.

RIP *Richard 'Dick' Baker* who passed away during the making of this cookbook. He and his kind wife Kath were a true inspiration and great air fryer friends, and without the two of you we would not have the international readership and knowledge we have today.

To *Julie*, thank you for your amazing friendship and inspiring me enough with your cookbook for me to make my own. You were the push that I needed and a great role model.

To my late *grandparents*, who started my love affair with great food. Your classic recipes fill many pages of this cookbook.

To *Smiths Butchers* for providing the best meat for Recipe This. For supplying us with every weird cut of meat we wanted and your sausages that are spectacular in the air fryer. To *Rafters Greengrocers* for your gorgeous fruit and veg boxes, and for supplying me with my first ever spaghetti squash, which I then air fried. I have loved shopping local and using both Smiths and Rafters in the recipe testing process of this cookbook.

To my *mum and dad* for being our biggest supporters and for your endless encouragement from day one. You even taste tested the first food we ever cooked in the air fryer. Thanks, Mum, for telling me to marry a chef, the only time I ever listened to you!

Chef Dom would personally like to thank the *Revelstoke Hotel*, Bridlington, who took him on as a pot washer at age of 14, later training him as a chef. For helping him when he was homeless and for caring. He would also like to thank John, Phil and Karen, who helped him through the early years of his career. Most importantly, Wendy, the teacher at college who was a truly wonderful woman and saw his potential.

# About the authors

Sam and Dom are the creators of the incredibly popular kitchen gadgets food blog Recipe This, which they started in the November of 2015. They have established themselves as the number one resource for recipes and advice for the air fryer, Instant Pot, Ninja Foodi, soup maker, slow cooker and many more.

They love creating kitchen gadget recipes that are easy prep, easy to cook and perfect for a busy lifestyle.

Sam and Dom are also mum and dad to Kyle, Sofia and Jorge and live in Yorkshire in the North of England.

**RecipeThis.com**